THE SECRETS OF
Provence

Publisher and Creative Director: Nick Wells
Project Editor: Cat Emslie
Picture Research: Cat Emslie and Victoria Lyle
Art Director: Mike Spender
Digital Design and Production: Chris Herbert
Layout Design: Theresa Maynard and Mike Spender

Special thanks to: Sara Robson, Victoria Lyle, Chelsea Edwards and Claire Walker

Picture Credits

All photographs courtesy of and © Hugh Palmer, except the following:
© Hugh Palmer, from *The Most Beautiful Villages of Provence* by Michael Jacobs (Thames & Hudson; London and New York, 1999):
36, 41, 42, 114, 122, 126, 140, 165, 177, 181; courtesy of Fotolia: 8, 66, 80, 101; courtesy of Shutterstock and the following photographers: Stefan Ataman 79;
Silvano Audisio 64; Denis Babenko 78; Gilles Barattini 146; Mauro Bighin 150; Vera Bogaerts 29; Thomas Pozzo di Borgo 76, 84; Bouzou 63, 100;
Dan Breckwoldt 6, 27, 28; Franck Camhi 5 (t), 103, 104; Ivan Cholakov 160; Claudio Giovanni Colombo 43, 67; Drserg 157; Dubassy 68, 77, 99;
Elena Elisseeva 59, 60, 106, 108; Alfito Ferlito 62; Douglas Freer 171; Karel Gallas 166; Andrej Gibasiewicz 4, 13, 30; David Hughes 16, 55, 98, 102, 117, 148, 153;
Philip Lange 4–5, 57, 58; Macumazahn 12, 15, 81, 85, 118; Titus Manea 172; Lazar Mihai-Bogdan 162; Tan Wei Ming 170; Patrick Morand 88;
Christian Musat 7, 82, 89, 90, 109, 110; Sean Nel 72, 73, 74, 149; Photazz 161; Suze Piat 135; Massimiliano Pieraccini 50; Olga Shelego 65;
Helen Shorey 91; Manfred Steinbach 152, 158; Vinicius Tupinamba 168; Graca Victoria 3, 159.

Metro Books
122 Fifth Avenue
New York, NY 10011

ISBN-13: 978-1-4351-1107-3

1 3 5 7 9 10 8 6 4 2

Printed and bound in China

THE SECRETS OF
Provence

Diane & Jon Sutherland

METRO BOOKS
NEW YORK

CONTENTS

Introduction   **6**

VAUCLUSE   **10**

Summit ridge, Mont Ventoux   12
Lavender field, near Sault   13
Towards the village, Aurel   14
Vineyard and peaks, Dentelles
    de Montmirail   16
View from Ouvèze River,
    Vaison-la-Romaine   17
Parish church, Vaison-la-Romaine   18
Medieval town, Vaison-la-Romaine   20
Towards the village, Crestet   21
Fountain, Crestet   22
Église St-Denis, Séguret   23
Poppy field, Séguret   24
Towards the village, Venasque   26
Pont St-Bénezét, Avignon   27
Palais des Papes, Avignon   28
Canal and bridge, L'Isle-sur-la-Sorgue   29
Abbaye Notre-Dame de Sénanque,
    near Gordes   30
Towards the town, Gordes   32

Towards the Coulon Valley, Gordes   34
Notre-Dame-d'Alydon, Oppède-le-Vieux   35
Roussillon, Plateau de Vaucluse   36
Ochre quarries, Roussillon   37
Parish church, Ménerbes   38
Castle gateway, Lacoste   39
Towards the village, Bonnieux   40
Église Neuve, Bonnieux   41
Pont Julien, near Bonnieux   42
Town houses and bunting, Apt   43
Château de Lourmarin, Lourmarin   44
Église SS-Andre et Trophime, Lourmarin   45
Château d'Ansouis, Ansouis   46
Église St-Martin, Ansouis   47

BOUCHES-DU-RHÔNE   **48**

Château du Roi René, Tarascon   50
Village and Église St-Vincent,
    Les Baux-de-Provence   51
Château des Baux, Les Baux-de-Provence   52
Towards the village, Eygalières   53
Chapelle des Pénitents, Eygalières   54
Chaîne des Alpilles, Crau Plain   55
Les Arènes, Nîmes   56
The Maison Carrée, Nîmes   58
Jardin de la Fontaine, Nîmes   59
Pont du Gard, near Nîmes   60
Les Arènes, Arles   62
Ramparts, Aigues-Mortes, the Camargue   63
Wild Horse, the Camargue   64
Bulls, the Camargue   65
Flamingos, the Camargue   66

Église St-Michel, Salon-de-Provence   67
Houses and boats on
    the Canal, Martigues   68
Abbaye de Silvacane, near la
    Roque-d'Anthéron   70
Roman aqueduct ruins, near Meyrargues   71
Tour de l'Horloge, Aix-en-Provence   72
Cathédrale St-Sauveur, Aix-en-Provence   73
Courtyard Fountain, Aix-en-Provence   74
Montagne Ste-Victoire,
    east of Aix-en-Provence   76
Church, L'Estaque   77
Vieux Port, Marseille   78
Cathédrale de la Nouvelle Major,
    Marseille   79
Château d'If, Île d'If, Marseille   80
Les Calanques, Gardiole Cliffs   81
Boats in the harbour, Cassis   82
Cap Canaille, east of Cassis   84
Sunset at the harbour, La Ciotat   85

VAR   **86**

Vineyards, Le Castellet   88
Harbour and promenade, Bandol   89
Harbour, Sanary-sur-Mer   90
Marina, Toulon   91
Village street, Fox-Amphoux   92
Village and Église St-Denis, Tourtour   93
Towards the village, Villecroze   94
Village and ruined towers, Cotignac   95
Village and Église St-Sauveur,
    Entrecasteaux   96

Presqu'île de Giens, near Hyères 98
City and Collégiale St-Paul, Hyères 99
Tour St-Blaise, Hyères 100
Îles d'Hyères, off the coast of Hyères 101
Harbour, Le Lavandou 102
Village street, Ramatuelle 103
Le Moulin de Paillas, near Ramatuelle 104
Boats docked in the harbour, St-Tropez 106
Pampelonne Beach, Baie de Pampelonne 108
Village and Église St-Michel, Grimaud 109
Château de Grimaud, Grimaud 110
Village and Castle Keep,
    Les Arcs-sur-Argens 111
Village and Église St-Michel, Ampus 112
Overlooking the village, Bargemon 114
Village and chateau, Trigance 115
Towards the village, Seillans 116
Baptistery of Cathédrale
    St-Léonce, Fréjus 117
Massif de l'Esterel, eastern Var coast 118

ALPES DE HAUTE-PROVENCE 120
Towards the village, Colmars-les-Alpes 122
Fort de France, Colmars-les-Alpes 124
Towards the village, Lurs 125
Notre-Dame-de-Vie, Lurs 126
Towards the village, Annot 128
Bridge over the River Vaire, Annot 129

Towards the village, Méailles 130
Steps in the village, Méailles 131
Church, Méailles 132
Town and citadel, Entrevaux 133
Cathédrale Notre-Dame-de,
    l'Assomption Entreveaux 134
Town and church, Moustiers-Ste-Marie 135
Ravin de Notre Dame, above
    Moustiers-Ste-Marie 136
Lavender, Plateau de Valensole 137
Riez, Plateau de Valensole 138
Chapelle Ste-Maxime, near Riez 140
Chapelle Ste-Maxime interior, near Riez 142
Grand Canyon du Verdon, between
    Casellane and Moustiers-Ste-Marie 143

ALPES-MARITIMES 144
Lake Trecolpas area, Parc National
    du Mercantour 146
La Croisette, Cannes 148
Skyline from harbour square, Cannes 149
Palais des Festivals, Cannes 150
Harbour and Fort Carré, Antibes 152
Village street, Haut-de-Cagnes 153
St-Paul-de-Vence, north of
    Cagnes-sur-Mer 154
Fruit market, St-Paul-de-Vence 155
Promenade des Anglais, Nice 156
Hôtel Negresco, Nice 158
Port area, Nice 159
Cathédrale Orthodoxe Russe, Nice 160
Bay view, Villefranche-sur-Mer 161
Villa Ephrussi de Rothschild,
    Cap Ferrat 162
Jardin d'Èze, Èze 164
Arched doorway, Èze 165

Port de Fontvielle, Fontvieille, Monaco 166
Palais Princier, Monaco-Ville, Monaco 168
Monaco Cathedral, Monaco-Ville,
    Monaco 170
Casino de Monte Carlo,
    Monte Carlo, Monaco 171
Towards the front, Menton 172
Towards the village, Peillon 174
Église St-Sauveur de la
    Transfiguration, Peillon 175
Village and Église Ste-Marguerite,
    Luceram 176
Chapelle St-Jean, Luceram 177
Towards the valley, from Luceram 178
Saorge, La Roya Valley 179
Stone building, Saorge 180
Couvent Franciscain, Saorge 181
Chapelle de la Madone del
    Poggio, Saorge 182
La Brigue, Levenza Valley 184
Collégiale St-Martin, La Brigue 185
Château des Lascaris watchtower,
    La Brigue 186
Chapelle Notre-Dame de Fontaines,
    La Brigue 188
Interior of the Chapelle Notre-Dame de
    Fontaines, La Brigue 189

Index 190

INTRODUCTION

Provence will cast its spell on you long before you set foot on its soil. Thousands of holidaymakers make their pilgrimage to this region in the south of France every summer; thousands more have made their homes there, drawn by TV documentary makers and the books written by Peter Mayle (b. 1939).

Some are drawn by the calm of the countryside, with vast expanses of purple lavender and golden sunflowers; others are attracted by the ancient towns and villages or the beauty of the lakes and the mountains. Provence always seems to be in soft focus, a playground loved by many since the Roman times.

Away from the areas of cultivation, the bustling and trendy centres, there is a rocky, rough and almost elemental land. It retains its primitiveness where you can still stand alone in the mountains or the crags. You can walk in the warmth of a hundred village markets, sip a pastis before lunch and understand why the locals favour a siesta.

Vaucluse, the first of the five departments (or *départements*) that make up the region, is steeped in history and culture. Avignon was once the home of the Popes that lived in the vast Gothic Papal palace with its huge, white walls. Mont Ventoux to the northeast is probably Provence's most identifiable landmark: it is a pyramid of rock that remains capped with snow for six months of the year. To the west are chalk ridges that look like lacework, with picturesque hamlets clinging to their sides. Close to these are the Côtes-du-Rhône wine villages, the best known

being Gigondas, Vacqueyras and Beaumes de Venise. In this region you will find the Luberon and its fashionable, perched villages. The houses seem to tumble down the hillsides and sit precariously on rocky ridges. There is a valley full of cedars imported from Morocco, and Ménerbes, where Peter Mayle wrote his first book.

Moving to the coast, the Bouches-du-Rhône boasts Provence's largest city, Marseille, the home of the Bouillabaisse, France's quintessential fish stew. In stark contrast is Aix-en-Provence,

more up-market and cultured and perhaps with the most elegant thoroughfares in Provence, with its huge plane trees, fountains and eighteenth-century townhouses. This was the home of Paul Cézanne (1839–1906) and eleven miles away is the chalk mountain, Montagne Ste-Victorie, which mesmerized him. Van Gogh (1853–90) stayed for a year in the St-Paul-de-Mausole asylum in St-Rémy-de-Provence at the end of the nineteenth century and painted over 150 pictures there. The region is also the home of Arles and the Camargue. At Arles there is a 20,000-seat bullring and to the south of the town lies the 200,000-acre flatland of the Camargue, famed for its white horses, pink flamingos and black bulls.

Var has a racy reputation borne out of its warmth, great beaches and tourist hotspots like St-Tropez. Its coast must be one of the most beautiful, but lively, regions in Europe: from St-Cyr to St-Raphael there are miles of sandy beaches, rocky coves and promenades dominated by dramatic mountain backdrops. In the summer the villages and ports in this region, each a patchwork of tiny streets and stairways, is tightly packed with visitors. Harbours and beaches are fringed with palms and pastel painted houses, overlooked by olive groves and vines. Beyond the hurly burly of the tourist resorts there are scented forests and clicking cicadas. Inland from the beaches are the steep-sided valleys of the Massif de Maures, with isolated hamlets and a dark, rock granite that seems to soak up the sunlight. Even further north, in Upper Var, are villages that were inaccessible by road until only seventy years ago.

The Alpes de Haute-Provence is considered by many to be the hard core of Provence. It is high, rocky and wild and the remoter areas are littered with abandoned farmhouses. It has become a playground for canoeists, climbers, trekkers and riders. Driving through the Gorges du Verdon is not something to be attempted if you suffer from vertigo. The Ubaye Valley offers excellent skiing in winter and river sports in the summer. The Mercantour National Park has larch forests, pines, rocky mountain tops and huge alpine meadows.

To the west lie the department of Alpes-Maritimes and the Côte d'Azur. The home of Cannes and Nice, the sun kisses these miles of coastline – also known as the French Riviera – for all but thirty or forty days of the year. It is hard to believe that less than 150 years ago Cannes was an unimportant fishing village and in modern times Nice has become France's fifth largest city. In the summer the Côte d'Azur is at its liveliest, with flower markets, festivals and a host of other cultural events. The landscape changes abruptly once you leave the coast: the roads twist and turn through the hills and mountains amidst a canopy of pines and thyme-scented air. Further north are the Alps, with their snowy peaks and famed skiing, merely an hour from the beaches.

in Europe, tiny fortified towns, precariously perched villages and great cities. The senses are assaulted by the warmth, the food, the wine and the aroma of the herbs and plants. It has attracted artists and recluses, the rich and the famous and has seen the Greeks, the Romans, the Saracens and the Italians pass through and put down their roots. Many describe Aix-en-Provence as a mini-Paris and Avignon as a mini-Rome.

Provence has its feet in the Mediterranean and its head in the Alps. It is a palette of colour with its fields of lavender, herbs, poppies, sunflowers and its skies of brilliant blue. The cooking is distinctive too from the rest of French cuisine. The Mediterranean influence brings with it hot spices and seafood; garlic, olive oil and olives are dominant, as are the abundant Herbes de Provence. Alexandre Dumas wrote:

'Provençal cooking is based on garlic. The air in Provence is impregnated with the aroma of garlic, which makes it very healthy to breathe. Garlic is the main seasoning in bouillabaisse and in the principle sauces of the region. A sort of mayonnaise is made with it by crushing it in oil, and this is eaten with fish and snails.'

Though not included here, the department of Hautes-Alpes, nestled alongside Italy and north of Alpes de Haute-Provence, is sometimes also considered part of the region. It is a land of valleys, canyons and mountains and is probably the least populated and least visited part of 'Provence', yet it has over thirty ski resorts and boasts hiking, horseback riding, mountain climbing, hangliding, kayaking and canoeing. The area is also home to the chamois and the ibex, and delicious mountain cheeses, herb flavoured honey and ripe apples can be bought in tiny villages 2,000 m (6,500 ft) above sea level.

For many, Provence is the most irresistible part of France; it truly has everything, from snowcapped mountains of the southern Alps to the plains of the Camargue, the most spectacular canyon

It was the Greeks that introduced the olive 2,500 years ago and whole markets are dedicated to the sale of strings of pale purple garlic. Provence has double or triple seasons to grow tomatoes, aubergines, courgettes and onions. Their cheeses are made from goat's or ewe's milk and the region is famed for its distinctive honey, its fruits and its nougat. There are also almonds, figs and an abundance of fish on the coast. The Côtes-du-Rhône region, which covers 171 communes in various departments including Provence's Bouches-du-Rhône and Vaucluse, produces some of France's finest wines.

Recent history has been kind to Provence: the Second World War barely impinged upon it and just twenty-five years ago the centralizing power of Paris that aimed to wipe out regional identities was reversed, bringing with it new dual signs and a celebration of regional importance. Avignon is just two and a half hours from Paris and the other major cities of the region are just three hours away from the capital city. The transport systems have transformed Marseille, now seen to be the most dynamic of French cities and which has just celebrated its 2,600th birthday.

Mercifully most of Provence remains as most would wish: the fruit basket of France, the home of lavender, olive oil and terracotta. Large areas are still under populated and many tiny villages still struggle to keep their single shops open. In stark contrast are the smart second homes and sprawling properties of rich foreigners. Tourism has imbalanced Provence, but out of season it returns to normality; an agricultural land, a land of contrast and beauty, a place where time, technology and money have barely touched or scratched the surface of its people's ways of life.

Provence is a magical part of France, which will fire one's imagination and delight the visitor. Steeped in art and history, and marinated in a mix of olive oil, lavender and wine, the region is a feast for all the senses; a place to relax amidst a landscape of peaceful towns, serene countryside, stunning and spectacular scenery and breathtaking, panoramic views. Delight in this book, which will dazzle you with some of the most celebrated sights and cities, alongside the little villages off the beaten track and corners of the region you have yet to discover.

VAUCLUSE

Vaucluse has a wealth of beautiful natural sites: hills, mountains, lavender fields, ochre cliffs, dramatic gorges and picturesque villages.

Situated in the northwest corner of Provence, much of this department dates back to Roman times. This is evidenced in Vaison-la-Romaine and the preserved Roman theatre in Orange. Near Bonnieux is the Pont Julien bridge and in Avignon is the Palais des Papes.

Vaucluse is bordered on the west by the River Rhône and to the south by the River Durance. The area is impressively scenically diverse, ranging from the limestone mountains of the Luberon to the white slopes of Mont Ventoux, which dominates the area, and the Alps sheltering the department to the north. Herbs, lavender, poppies and wheat fields, not to mention the wild flowers, fill the landscape with colour.

Picturesque villages like Lacoste, Gordes, Roussillon, Ménerbes and Apt are perched on hillsides; there are stunningly superb views from mountain ridges and walks with outstanding photographic opportunities, winding, narrow, cobbled streets and chateaux and churches that dominate the skyline. The villages often have colourful, tree-shaded squares where such gastronomic delights as fresh cherries, melons, strawberries and locally produced wine and cheese can be enjoyed.

SUMMIT RIDGE
Mont Ventoux

Mont Ventoux is the largest mountain in Vaucluse, nicknamed the 'Giant of Provence' and 'The Bald Mountain'. It lies west of the Luberon range and to the east of the jagged Dentelles de Montmirail. The summit – which is buffeted by the winds of the northerly mistral – is bare limestone, with little vegetation, giving the impression throughout the year of a snow-capped mountain. It dominates the region, overlooking the Rhône Valley and the view is breathtaking. Protected by UNESCO (United Nations Educational, Scientific and Cultural Organization), Mont Ventoux is on the route of the Tour de France.

LAVENDER FIELD
near Sault

The immense blue-purple fields of lavender near the health resort of Sault are a sight for sore eyes. One of the French sites chosen for protection by UNESCO, the city of Sault is one of the stops on the lavender tour because of its beauty. Perched at 776 m (2,546 ft) altitude, Sault holds its biggest lavender festival in August each year. One of the main products that Sault produces, in addition to lavender, is lavender honey, together with macaroons and nougat. The superb views from Sault encompass the vivid fields of lavender, alternating with fields of wheat.

TOWARDS THE VILLAGE
Aurel

The beautiful village of Aurel is situated near the borders of
Vaucluse, Drôme and the Alpes de Haute-Provence.
Surrounded by wild, mountainous countryside, at the base of
Mont Ventoux, the village is delightful. The narrow streets
and ancient stone houses are clustered around the twelfth-
century church of Ste Aurèle. In the village there are also the
remains of a twelfth-century chateau. Known for the quality
of its light and superb views of fields of lavender, Aurel is
popular with painters and for earthenware and pottery.

VINEYARD AND PEAKS
Dentelles de Montmirail

Extending from the Ventoux mountains, the Dentelles de Montmirail are short, steep mountains, whose sharp peaks in their distinctive rocky ridge, eroded by the mistral, are said to resemble lace (*dentelle*). The range is forested with pine and oak woods on the lower slopes and the surrounding land is rich in truffles and lavender. The River Ouvèze flows by the northern edge of the Dentelles and the Rhône flows to the west, making this fertile part of the Vaucluse a part of the Côtes-de-Rhône wine area.

VIEW FROM OUVÈZE RIVER
Vaison-la-Romaine

The ancient town of Vaison-la-Romaine sits high on the banks of the Ouvèze River. The single-arched Roman Bridge just visible here to the left is still in regular use after 2,000 years. Vaison-la-Romaine has a large collection of ancient ruins and the bridge joins the two parts of the town. In the Quartier Puymin the Villa des Messii, Portique du Pompey and a Roman theatre can be found, while in the Quartier de la Villasse are many excavated streets, houses and baths. Vaison-la-Romaine is renowned for its music and dance festivals and theatre.

PARISH CHURCH
Vaison-la-Romaine

This fifteenth-century (dating from 1464, but expanded in
the eighteenth century) parish church stands halfway up the
Haute Ville (upper town) area of Vaison-la-Romaine, which
sits on a high rock to the south of the river and is full of
narrow, medieval streets and small squares. In addition to the
Haute Ville and the Puymin and la Villasse archaeological
sites, are the cathedral of Notre-Dame-de-Nazareth and the
St-Quenin chapel. In 1950 an unearthed sarcophagus
contained what was thought to be the remains of St Quenin,
a sixth-century bishop of Vaison. The cathedral's eleventh-
century white marble altar is adorned with grapes, the
emblem of Vaison-la-Romaine.

MEDIEVAL TOWN
Vaison-la-Romaine

The medieval town of Vaison-la-Romaine boasts the ruined castle of the Counts of Toulouse (seen on the left). In the twelfth century the Counts, who ruled over the Comtat Venaissin, built a chateau on the hill in the fortified town. The bishops then began a conflict that lasted for a hundred years. During the thirteenth and fourteenth centuries many of the population moved, for safety during the Hundred Years War, from the north side of the river to the base of the chateau. The castle fell into disrepair during the French Revolution.

TOWARDS THE VILLAGE
Crestet

The village of Crestet is perched on a crest at the north edge of the Dentelles de Montmirail, facing Mont Ventoux. Its charming, narrow streets lead to a twelfth-century chateau, which was the former residence of the bishops of Vaison-la-Romaine and their refuge during their conflict with the Counts of Toulouse. Crestet also has an eleventh-century church, of St Sauveur, and the Stahly foundation, which is the former home of the sculptor François Stahly, as well as breathtaking, panoramic views of Mont Ventoux and the Dentelles de Montmirail.

FOUNTAIN
Crestet

ÉGLISE ST-DENIS
Séguret

The old fountain in Crestet's minute village square is in front of the old church. In order to allow visitors to the church to see the inside of it, it has an iron grille over its entrance. The village's washing trough is also still visible, accessed through the archway at the side of the church. Crestet's narrow, cobbled streets make investigation by foot most appropriate. An orientation table allows the visitor to identify the different peaks, hills, crests and valleys in the spectacular views from the village.

Séguret's Romanesque-style parish church originated in the tenth century, but was renovated during the eleventh and twelfth centuries. Séguret is typically and charmingly Provençal in nature. The Rue des Poternes is lined with ancient houses and a Huguenot gate retains two of its ironbound wooden shutters. The stunning views from Séguret include its neighbouring village of Sablet, sitting in the middle of the plain. Séguret is situated on the western side of the Dentelles de Montmirail, at the foot of a hill boasting a ruined chateau.

POPPY FIELD
Séguret

The approach to the hillside village of Séguret is lined with poppy fields and vineyards. The village is famous for its own Côtes-du-Rhone-Villages AOC wine. Séguret's wine-making tradition dates back several centuries, beginning with the Counts of Toulouse. The vineyards changed hands several times over the centuries and the wine-makers made Séguret a free district in the twelfth century, taking control of their own destiny. The Roaix-Séguret wine cellar is one of the area's vineyard cooperatives, with neighbouring village Roaix, formed in 1685.

TOWARDS THE VILLAGE
Venasque

Venasque lies on the western edge of the Plateau de Vaucluse. This picturesque village is perched on the summit of a rocky outcrop and dominates the Nesque valley and the plain of Carpentras. Small and compact and surrounded by lush greenery, Venasque is one of the 126 'most beautiful villages in France' and one of the oldest villages of the Comtat Venaissin. The twelfth-century church of Notre Dame (the spire of which can be seen here) has a high bell tower and gargoyles, and the town is host to attractive eighteenth-century fountains. The panoramic views from the ancient Saracen towers are spectacular.

PONT ST-BÉNEZÉT
Avignon

Famously the subject of the song 'Sur le Pont d'Avignon', the Pont St-Bénezét in Avignon was built in the twelfth century; only four of the original twenty-two arches remain today. According to legend, St Bénezét, a shepherd boy, was 'commanded by angels' to build a bridge, and his show of strength in lifting a block of stone inspired the bridge's construction. On his death he was interred in a small chapel that stands on the second pier. This chapel (of St Nicholas) also became the place of worship for Rhône boatmen.

PALAIS DES PAPES
Avignon

The gigantic Palais des Papes took twenty years to construct
from 1335 and was primarily built on the instruction of
Pope Benedict XII and expanded by Popes Clement VI
(1291–1352), Innocent VI (1282/95–1363) and Urban V
(1310–70). The largest Gothic palace in the world, it remained
under papal control for 350 years. It was sacked during the
French Revolution (1789) and subsequently taken over by the
Napoleonic French as a military base and a prison. In 1906
the Palais des Papes became a national museum and so
began its restoration.

CANAL AND BRIDGE
L'Isle-sur-la-Sorgue

A picturesque island town in the middle of the river Sorgue,
l'Isle-sur-la-Sorgue has several canals running through its centre.
Lying at the foot of the Plateau de Vaucluse, in the plains of
Comtat Venaissin, l'Isle-sur-la-Sorgue is steeped in history. The
canals, which once provided power via a series of waterwheels,
are crisscrossed by tiny bridges, which run between the narrow,
ancient streets. The church of Notre-Dame-des-Anges has a
baroque interior and several impressive mansions have been
converted into art galleries, including Maison René Char. The
town is also famous for antique fairs.

ABBAYE NOTRE-DAME DE SÉNANQUE
near Gordes

A valley of lavender fields stretch out from the Cistercian Abbaye-de-Sénanque buildings. The abbey was founded in the twelfth century and sits in the deep Sénancole valley. Cistercian until the sixteenth century, the Vaudois revolted in 1544, hanging the monks and destroying many buildings. The abbey changed hands several times during the following centuries, particularly during the French Revolution and anti-monastic laws of the nineteenth century. Since the 1970s, the patronage of the Association des Amis de Sénanque, means monks again live there permanently.

TOWARDS THE TOWN
Gordes

The view of Gordes is dominated by its church, the
Église St-Fermin, and the chateau. The imposing chateau
was built in the sixteenth century on the site of a former
twelfth-century fortification. It has a Renaissance fireplace
and entrance door, but retains its distinctive twelfth-century
machicolated corner tower, and today is the home of the
Musée Pol Mara. Pol Mara (1920–98) was a contemporary
Flemish painter who lived in Gordes. There are concerts
in the chateau's courtyard in summer and many artists,
musicians and politicians spend their holidays in Gordes.

TOWARDS THE COULON VALLEY
from Gordes

Spectacular views of the Coulon Valley are seen from the ancient stone houses and walls of the village of Gordes, perched on a ridge of the southern slopes of the Plateau de Vaucluse. West of Gordes is an area containing beehive-shaped dry-stone huts called *bories*. Village des Bories was inhabited until the early nineteenth century, possibly by shepherds. The walls of the *bories* are up to four feet thick. This is thought to be the largest collection, some 3,000 in total, although they are also visible throughout the Vaucluse area.

NOTRE-DAME-D'ALYDON
Oppède-le-Vieux

The church of Notre-Dame-d'Alydon, with its gargoyled, hexagonal bell tower, can be found in the upper part of this magnificent little hilltop village. Once used as a fortification, the Romanesque church (rebuilt in the sixteenth century) looms above the houses and cobbled streets. Some frescoes remain intact inside the church, which is currently being renovated by the locals. Just above the church are the crumbling and precarious ruins of a twelfth-century chateau (a gap in its walls allows the view shown here). Views from the village across the plateau to Ménerbes are breathtaking.

ROUSSILLON
Plateau de Vaucluse

The ochre-red village of Roussillon, classified as one of the 'most beautiful villages in France', is set in a pine forest on the southern edge of the Plateau de Vaucluse. It has a nineteenth-century clock-and-bell tower, with ancient sundials and topped by a wrought-iron belfry and campanile bell. The village is small with colourful old buildings and narrow, medieval streets. Roussillon's charm lies mainly in its colours: red, brown and ochre cliffs and quarries, green pine forests and azure skies.

OCHRE QUARRIES
Roussillon

The natural park of cliffs and quarries of ochre lie around the village of Roussillon and are thought to have been used since prehistoric times. This area of ochre is the largest in the world and the disused open-air quarries can be visited along the Sentier des Ocres (Ochre Path). Used as a natural dye, the ochre was exported all over the world until the end of the nineteenth century. Within the town of Roussillon is located an old ochre factory, now containing the Conservatoire des Ocres et des Pigments Appliqués.

PARISH CHURCH
Ménerbes

Ménerbes' fourteenth-century parish church is perched on the east end of the village. In fact Ménerbes lies, west to east, across the top of a long wooded ridge that overlooks vineyards. In addition to the church it has the old chateau du Castellet at the western end, a sixteenth-century citadel and an eighteenth-century *mairie*, or town hall, with a wrought-iron belfry in a tiny late-Rennaissance square. The views from the arch beside the *mairie* span from Gordes in the north to the ancient abbey of St-Hilaire to the east.

CASTLE GATEWAY
Lacoste

The cobbled streets of Lacoste give the impression that time has stood still in this charming medieval village. It is situated to the east of a mountain spine that rises between the Plateau de Vaucluse and Luberon and faces Bonnieux to the east. The ruined chateau of the Marquis de Sade (1740–1814) is at the top of the village and dates to the sixteenth and eighteenth centuries, although some of the walls that still remain are twelfth century. The oldest building is the ninth-century Maison Forte.

TOWARDS THE VILLAGE
Bonnieux

Bonnieux is one of the largest and most impressive of the Luberon villages. Eighty-six steps lead to the twelfth-century Roman-Gothic church above the village, which is known as the 'Vielle Église', or old church. Its altitude of 425 m (1,395 ft) provides spectacular views of Monts de Vaucluse and Mont Ventoux, Lacoste, Gordes and Roussillon across the cherry orchards, forests and vineyards of the plateau. On the road to Lourmarin when leaving Bonnieux is a man-made cedar forest, originating from seeds from the Atlas Mountains in Morocco, sown in 1861.

ÉGLISE NEUVE
Bonnieux

In 1870, in line with the Bonnieux population's migration down the hill, the old *haute église* was replaced by a new neo-Romanesque church, or 'Église Neuve', lower down in the village. The new church now houses classical music concerts in July. Bonnieux has a history of opulence, with the houses dating back to the sixteenth century when bishops lived in the village, which belonged to the Popes of Avignon. Also of note is the Musée de la Boulangerie, contained in a seventeenth-century village house in Rue de la République.

PONT JULIEN
near Bonnieux

The Pont Julien is 5 km (3 miles) to the north of Bonnieux and is one of the best-preserved Roman bridges of the region – it is still used as a road. It is 80 m (263 ft) long and has three arches, the central one of which is higher than the others. The high archways were built in anticipation of high water levels and openings on either side of the arches allowed high water to pass through the bridge. Pont Julien was built from limestone quarries in Luberon and originally dates to 300 BC. Its name is thought to derive from the nearby town of Apta Julia (now Apt).

TOWN HOUSES AND BUNTING
Apt

Apt is a bustling market town that was an important Gallo-Roman city. With its long, narrow streets and tree-filled squares, Apt is famous for wine production, basket and wicker work, as well as its long-established reputation for hat making. It is also known worldwide for its candied fruit which is manufactured by Aptunion. Situated in the Luberon Nature Reserve, Apt also boasts the old Cathédrale Ste-Anne, now a parish church, and a baroque hotel, as well as a museum containing sculptures, paintings, stained glass windows and ceramics.

CHÂTEAU DE LOURMARIN
Lourmarin

This fifteenth- and sixteenth-century chateau was built by the Agoult family and has large Renaissance windows and a square tower. Inside the chateau are a cantilevered staircase and a Renaissance fireplace, distinctive because of its Corinthian and Indian figurines. Lourmarin is one of the largest Luberon villages with typical Mediterranean architecture, winding narrow streets and shaded public squares. The 1957 winner of the Nobel Prize for Literature, Albert Camus (1913–60), wrote and lived on the edge of the village of Lourmarin. He is buried in the Lourmarin cemetery.

ÉGLISE SS-ANDRE ET TROPHIME
Lourmarin

Lourmarin's eleventh-century church of St Andrew and St Trophime was renovated during the fourteenth and sixteenth centuries. Although little remains of the original features, the sixteenth-century Chapel of the Lord is still visible. It was renovated in the sixteenth century by the Agoult family, who ruled the area during the Papal times. It was used as a Protestant church until the seventeenth century, when it became a Catholic church again. The church has Gothic vaulting and is reached through the narrow, winding cobbled roads of Lourmarin.

CHÂTEAU D'ANSOUIS
Ansouis

The medieval Château d'Ansouis was originally built as a
hilltop fortification but has evolved over the years. It still retains
some of its fortified walls and watchtowers, as well as some
battlements. The beautiful gardens around the chateau are
decorated with carvings and the view from the terrace to the
mountain ridge of Ste Victoire is excellent. Inside the chateau is
a collection of seventeenth- and eighteenth-century furniture, as
well as some impressive tapestries. Now an estate house, the
chateau is classified as a *site et monument historique*.

ÉGLISE ST-MARTIN
Ansouis

The twelfth-century parish church of St Martin is built
amongst the houses of Ansouis and has a beautiful half-round
bell tower that dates from the sixteenth century. Ansouis itself
sits atop on a low hill and many of its stone buildings have been
restored. During the Middle Ages Ansouis was in a prime
position to control the road between Aix-en-Provence and
Apt and the location of the village protects it from the mistral.
The village square is shaded with plane trees and Ansouis is
full of small gardens.

BOUCHES-DU-RHÔNE

One of the first of the eighty-three original departments created in 1790 after the French Revolution, Bouches-du-Rhône was reduced in size when Vaucluse was created.

As the name implies, this department is situated where the River Rhône meets the Mediterranean Sea. It incorporates the expansive, flat wetland plains of the Camargue, with its vast protected park, its wild white horses, its bulls and its flamingos, and the Alpilles mountain range, which rises from the Rhône Valley. Marseille, Arles, Nîmes and Aix-en-Provence all have their own, sometimes spectacular, relics of the past, from Roman arenas to churches and chateaux.

No wonder then that the landscape varies dramatically in this part of Provence, with the changing colours of the sea, the different rock formations in the mountain ranges, the white of the beaches and the turquoise waters of Les Calanques. No wonder also that the area has attracted famous painters, such as Paul Cézanne (1839–1906) and his many impressions of Montagne Ste-Victoire, and Vincent Van Gogh (1853–90), who lived for many years in Arles. The city of Marseille is France's second-largest city and its largest commercial port, and Aix-en-Provence has a reputation for being the city of art, light and activity.

CHÂTEAU DU ROI RENÉ
Tarascon

The fabulous fortress-like, white-walled Château du Roi René was begun in 1400 by Louis II of Anjou (1377–1417), and finished in 1449 by his son, 'Good King René' (1409–80). René, the former King of Naples and Duke of Anjou, lavished the castle with fine items, such as the spiral staircases, painted ceilings and tapestries. It is protected on the banks of the River Rhône by a deep moat. The ancient, fortified town of Tarascon is nestled around the castle and also boasts medieval arcades, fifteenth-century cloisters and a twelfth- to fourteenth-century church, the Collegiale Ste-Marthe.

VILLAGE AND ÉGLISE ST-VINCENT
Les Baux-de-Provence

The view across the rooftops of les Baux-de-Provence, with the Alpilles range in the distance, shows the squat steeple of the Romanesque church of St Vincent, which is one of the oldest monuments in les Baux. One nave, dating back to the tenth century, is the oldest part of the church. A Romanesque-style nave and another with a Gothic edifice are also present. On the south face of the church, a circular turret topped with a dome is decorated with a gargoyle; a burning flame was traditionally lit here after a death in the village.

CHÂTEAU DES BAUX
Les Baux-de-Provence

The Château des Baux is a medieval fortress site that has been modified and restored at various times during the twelfth, thirteenth and sixteenth centuries. The castle site is host to its former chapel, of Ste Catherine, which is built into the walls of the fortress, as well as a dovecote. The town of Les Baux-de-Provence dominates the Alpilles, a craggy and barren mountainous rocky range that stretches from the River Rhône to the River Durance. The word *baux* means prominent cliff and this area of Provence has become famous for its mining of bauxite.

TOWARDS THE VILLAGE
Eygalières

Eygalières is set on top of a small hill and is surrounded by the olive groves, valleys and vineyards of the Alpilles. The remains of the castle, which can be identified by the statue of the Virgin as its crowning glory, and the tiny houses of the village can be seen from some distance, sitting atop the hill. The houses cling together along the narrow, winding streets, the main of which leads you up to the village church. Close by are the chateau ruins and the esplanade of the old gatehouse and St-Laurent church.

CHAPELLE DES PÉNITENTS
Eygalières

The Chapelle des Pénitents in Eygalières is home to the Musée Maurice Pezet, or the museum of old Eygalières, which has displays illuminating the archeological and ethnographical past of the village, from prehistory to more recent times, with prehistoric relics and agricultural tools on show. The chapel site also affords stunning views across to Mont Caume, the Alpilles and the River Durance. The name Eygalières itself is derived from the latin *aqualeria*, meaning 'that which collects water', which would certainly explain the verdant setting of this delightful little village.

CHAÎNE DES ALPILLES
Crau Plain

The Chaîne des Alpilles is a smaller extension of the Luberon range of mountains. The peaks and range itself are mostly bare limestone rock and scrub, but the lower slopes are rich in olive groves, pine trees, almond trees and the Kermes oak tree. Some of the species living in the nature reserve at the highest points of the range were introduced in the 1980s. They include Egyptian vultures, eagle owls and Bonelli's eagles. The Crau Plain stretches for about 50 kilometers from north to south. It experiences a range of climates and is popular with birdwatchers.

LES ARÈNES
Nîmes

This Roman amphitheatre was built between AD 90 and 120, and later fortified by the Visigoths. It was re-conquered by the French kings in the early eighteenth century, and the viscounts of Nîmes constructed a fortified palace within its walls. Seven hundred people lived within the arena during its service as an enclosed community and constructed two chapels. It was renovated during the nineteenth century for use as a bullring and Nîmes still holds regular bullfights there. Despite being part of the Gard department, Nîmes is effectively part of the region as it shares much Provençal and Gallo-Roman heritage.

THE MAISON CARRÉE
Nîmes

The Maison Carrée is situated behind the Arènes. It was built in *c.* 19–16 BC by Marcus Vipsanius Agrippa (63–13 BC) and was dedicated to his sons, Gaius and Lucius, adopted sons of Emperor Augustus (63 BC–AD 14) who had both died very young. The temple stands on Rue Auguste, the former site of the Roman forum and is constructed from local limestone, with a frieze of acanthus scrolls, thought to be from Rome. To the north of the Maison Carrée is a creation of glass and aluminium, the Carré d'Art, by British architect Norman Foster (b. 1935).

JARDIN DE LA FONTAINE
Nîmes

Situated in the northwest of Nîmes, the Jardin de la Fontaine provides peaceful and quiet walks through pine and cedar trees, stone terraces and lawns. The garden was named after the eighteenth-century fountain contained in a pond and was built on the site of the sacred Nemausus spring. Both the Temple of Diana and the Tour Magne, which is located at the top of Mont Cavalier, are Roman in origin. The large, octagonal Tour Magne, which stands 34 m (112 ft) high, was presented to Nîmes by Emperor Augustus in 15 BC.

PONT DU GARD
near Nîmes

Between Nîmes and Avignon, the Pont du Gard has been on the UNESCO World Heritage list since 1985 and is part of a Roman aqueduct built around AD 50. The bridge is 360 m (1,180 ft) long, almost 50 m (160 ft) high and is on three levels, the uppermost of which is composed of 47 arches. It is, as poetically put by its very own website, 'a water crossroads: where the aqueduct that snakes through the dense green countryside surges out onto the Pont du Gard to cross the Gardon river, leaving its gorges and heading down the plains to flow into the Rhône.'

LES ARÈNES
Arles

The amphitheatre (les Arenès) in Arles was built around the first century and was capable of accommodating 30,000 people. During the middle ages four towers were built and it was used as a fortification, containing houses and two chapels. It is one of the best preserved Roman arenas in France and every year it holds 20,000 people during the Easter Festival (La Féria) while bull fights (*corridas*) take place there. Arles is also famous for being the home of Vincent Van Gogh for a particularly impassioned and prolific 15 months of his life.

RAMPARTS
Aigues-Mortes, the Camargue

Construction of the city walls of medieval Aigues-Mortes began under Philippe le Hardi (1245–85), and was finished at the beginning of the fourteenth century by his son, Philippe le Bel (1268–1314). Built from limestone from Beaucaire and Les Baux de Provence, the ramparts are complete with gateways and circular towers, the most impressive of which is the Tour de Constance, built under Louis IX's (1214–70) reign. Also in Aigues-Mortes is the 1182 Église Notre-Dame-des-Sablons, recorded as Louis' place of prayer before setting off on his crusades.

WILD HORSE
the Camargue

These wild, white horses are found on the wetlands and salt marshes of the vast Rhône delta that is the natural haven of the Camargue. Possibly descended from prehistoric horses that lived during the Paleolithic period, this ancient breed can withstand the Camargue's bleak, cold winters and hot summers. They are the traditional mount of the guardians, or the 'Camargue cowboys' who herd the Camargue bulls that are used in bullfighting throughout France. Traditionally they are short-necked, deep-chested and compact, and they are calm, agile and intelligent.

BULLS
the Camargue

This specialized breed of bull runs semi-wild in the Camargue area of Provence. Smaller than most common breeds, they are raised for their meat and are used in a form of bullfighting that dates back to the sixteenth century. During the bullfight (or *course*) men known as '*razeteurs*' attempt to collect a rosette or tassel from between the horns of the bull. The bulls are the stars of these spectacles and they gain fame and statues in their honour. In the *Courses Camarguaises* the animals are not killed, unlike in the Spanish-style *corridas* that are also held.

FLAMINGOS
the Camargue

The emblem of the Camargue, this is the only place in France, and only one of a few in the whole Mediterranean area, where the pink flamingos nest. With a population of some 20,000 pairs living in the Camargue, the flamingos build their nests out of mud and mainly eat plankton by sucking it through their bills and filtering it in their mouths. It is the plankton, or crustacea, that gives the flamingo its distinctive pink plumage. This large species of flamingo lays a single, chalky-white egg on a mound of mud.

ÉGLISE ST-MICHEL
Salon-de-Provence

This thirteenth-century church has a Romanesque tympanum, or semi-circular, decorative wall, which displays the paschal lamb. Salon-de-Provence is one of the oldest villages in Provence and is surrounded by idyllic countryside, predominantly with olive trees. It is built on a small foothill and manufactures the soap 'Savon de Marseilles'. The village is also well known as being the home of Nostradamus (1503–66), the famous clairvoyant scholar, for many years. His house is now a museum detailing his life and personality in the old part of the village.

HOUSES AND BOATS ON THE CANAL
Martigues

The colourful village houses that line the Canal Saint-Sébastien are the former homes of seventeenth-century fishermen. Martigues is situated beside the lake, Étang de Berre, and is linked to the Mediterranean Sea by the Caroute Channel. Understandably, the picturesque and colourful houses have inspired many painters, including Duffy and Ziem. Martigues is known as 'The Venice of Provence' because of its canals and is virtually split into three different sections, L'isle, where the canals split, Ferrières in the north and Jonquières to the south.

ABBAYE DE SILVACANE
Near la Roque-d'Anthéron

Set in a completely serene and atmospheric location in fields on the southern banks of the Durance, the Abbaye de Silvacane is the youngest of the three Cistercian abbeys in Provence, built in 1144. Designed to be austere and functional, devoid of any ornament that would be likely to distract the monks from their prayers, it is considered one of the best examples of Cistercian architecture of the era. The harmonious building was acquired in 1846 by the state and is being restored. It is used for piano and music concerts, including the International String Quartet Festival.

ROMAN AQUEDUCT RUINS
near Meyrargues

This Roman aqueduct once served the town of Aix-en-Provence and is situated in the Durance Valley, in a hollow below the town of Meyrargues. This medieval town is home to an impressive and prominent feudal chateau, which overlooks the village from a rocky outcrop. Views from the chateau, with its huge and monumental stone staircase and large balustrade terrace, are superb over the valley. The chateau was renovated in the seventeenth century and is now a luxury hotel, although its 2-m (6½-ft) thick walls are still decorated in seventeenth- and eighteenth-century style.

TOUR DE L'HORLOGE
Aix-en-Provence

The clock tower on the corner of Aix-en-Provence's classical
Italianate, mid-seventeenth century Hôtel de Ville was built in
1510, with an astronomic clock dating from 1661. The town
hall itself houses many valuable manuscripts in its library and
boasts distinctive wood workings. In the same delightful square
is the highly decorated eighteenth-century Halle aux Grains
(corn exchange). Nearby are the Aquae Sextiae, thermal springs,
which were the reason the Romans first visited Aix-en-
Provence. An eighteenth-century spa was built on the site of the
ancient Roman baths of Sextius.

CATHÉDRALE ST-SAUVEUR
Aix-en-Provence

Built on the site of an ancient Roman road in the medieval part
of Aix-en-Provence, is the Cathédrale St-Sauveur. Its various
elements date from the fifth to the nineteenth centuries and as
such it is richly decorated, including some Gothic-style,
elaborately carved walnut doors. Inside are sixteenth-century
tapestries and a fourth-century baptismal pool. Adjoining the
cathedral are an archbishop's palace and a Romanesque cloister.
Medieval Aix-en-Provence was protected by a wall with thirty-
nine towers, one of which, the Tourreluquo Tower, remains in
the northwest of the town.

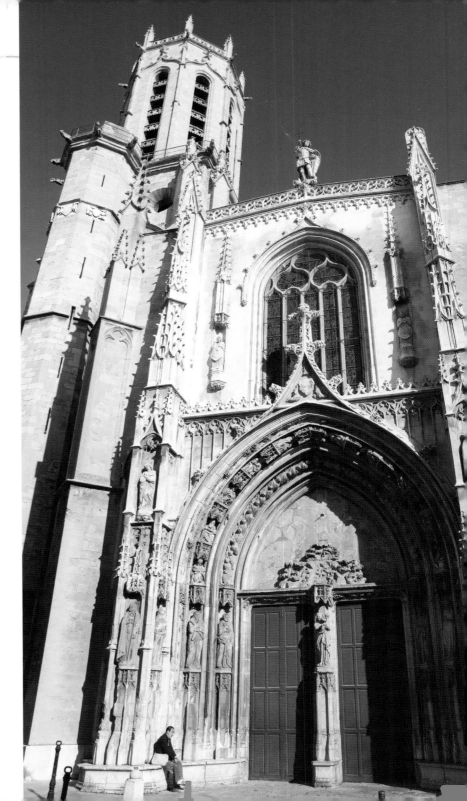

COURTYARD FOUNTAIN
Aix-en-Provence

This is just one of the many ornate fountains that decorate the streets and courtyards of Aix-en-Provence, often referred to as 'The City of a Thousand Fountains'. The heart of the Mazarin quarter boasts the seventeenth-century Fontaine des Quatre Dauphins, built by Jean-Claude Rambot (1621–94). The central Cours Mirabeau has several: la fontaine des Neuf Canons; a nineteenth-century fountain depicting 'Good King René' holding a bunch of grapes; a Roman, moss-covered, natural hot water spring; and the monumental La Rotonde, with three giant statues, representing art, justice and agriculture.

MONTAGNE STE-VICTOIRE
east of Aix-en-Provence

Dominating the landscape, this white limestone ridge runs from west to east and towers above Aix-en-Provence. With white cliffs on the southern edge and thick forest on the northern, it is not surprising that this landscape inspired many of Paul Cézanne's paintings, particularly incorporating the red soil at the foot of the mountain. The area in which Cézanne would regularly paint – he is thought to have produced around eighty works there – lies between Aix-en-Provence and the hamlet of Le Tholonet and is now known as the *Route Cézanne*.

CHURCH
L'Estaque

The prominent, whitewashed tower of the church of l'Estaque overlooks the tiny harbour. This tiny fishing village lies to the west of Marseille and belongs to the commune of that city. The view of the bay from the village itself has been depicted by many artists, but most famously by Paul Cézanne, who had a room in l'Estaque and portrayed the waters and the village through the changing seasons. In addition to the fishing port there is a small beach on the road to Martigues, which is popular with Marseille residents and visitors.

VIEUX PORT
Marseille

The hub of Marseille, the Vieux Port's inlet was used as a landing site by the Phocaean ships in 600 BC, and the quays were built by Kings Louis XII (1462–1515) and XIII (1601–43). Perched high on top of la Colline de la Garde (Garde Hill) and affording magnificent views over the bay and city, is the Notre-Dame de la Garde basilica. Built on the site of a thirteenth-century chapel and a sixteenth-century fortification against the Spanish, the basilica itself was erected between 1853 and 1899. Its 18-m (60-ft) high belfry is topped with a gilded statue of the Virgin.

CATHÉDRALE DE LA NOUVELLE MAJOR
Marseille

The large Romano-Byzantine-style Cathédrale de la Nouvelle Major, located on the north side of the old town, by the modern docks, was built between 1852 and 1893. It has spectacular domes, 444 marble columns supporting the roof and the tombs of the Bishops of Marseille lie in the crypt. The Ancienne Cathédrale de la Major dates to the eleventh century – Romanesque in style, part of it still remains to the side of the new cathedral, but during the nineteenth century much of it was demolished to accommodate its new and impressive successor.

CHÂTEAU D'IF
Île d'If, Marseille

Set on an island, the Île d'If, in the bay of Marseille is the Château d'If. It was built in the early sixteenth century and consists of a fort, a church and a guardhouse. From 1634 the chateau was used as a prison and during the Second World War the Germans occupied it for its strategic position. Although the chateau is sparse and uninviting – unsurprising given its history – the views from Île d'If to Marseille are stunning. The chateau was of course made internationally famous by the 1844 novel *The Count of Monte Cristo*, by Alexandre Dumas (1802–70).

LES CALANQUES
Gardiole Cliffs

These deep, narrow inlets in the rocky white cliffs lie between Cassis and Marseilles on the coast of Provence. They were formed by the rivers that flowed into the sea and by the rising level of the Mediterranean Sea. Some of the long, narrow inlets have tiny harbours, providing many a sailor with a safe haven during stormy weather. A few even have small beaches at the end of the inlets. Scuba divers, rock climbers, pleasure seekers and nature lovers find the pristine turquoise coves of Les Calanques a bewitching and magical place.

BOATS IN THE HARBOUR
Cassis

The tiny, ancient fishing port of Cassis has a very pretty harbour area and a few small beaches to either side of the port. Cassis village was rebuilt on its ruins during the eighteenth century; however it still retains some buildings that date from the sixteenth century. Many have been restored using the pastel colours of Provence. The fourteenth-century Château de Cassis, which was the property of the Baux family until 1426 but is now a hotel, overlooks the harbour. Cassis became famous for its stone, which was used around the world and in the Statue of Liberty in America.

CAP CANAILLE
east of Cassis

Rising to a maximum height of 394 m (1,290 ft), at la 'Grande Tête', Cap Canaille is one of Europe's highest maritime cliffs. Whereas the cliffs of Les Calanques are made of white limestone, those of Cap Canaille are made of yellow sandstone, which is rich in sea fossils and consequently they are famous for their reddish colours at sunset. Spectacular views, if a little precarious, can be had from the cape, with La Ciotat on one side, to the east, and the Gulf of Cassis and the tiny island of Riou on the other, to the west.

SUNSET AT THE HARBOUR
La Ciotat

The old fishing port of La Ciotat, surrounded by seventeenth-century houses, can be viewed spectacularly from the coastal road of the Route des Crêtes. A neo-Renaissance-style building dating from 1864, on Quai Ganteaume, houses the museum of l'Association des Amis du Vieux La Ciotat (Musée Ciotaden). La Ciotat became famous in 1895 when the Lumière brothers gave the first public screening of a projected motion picture at L'Eden, today the world's oldest surviving cinema. Also, in 1907 a man named Jules Lenoir invented the game of pétanque in La Ciotat, with the first tournament in 1910.

VAR

The coastline of the Var department stretches for some 430 km (270 miles), from Bandol in the west to the wilderness of the Massif de l'Esterel in the east, and the region has an average of 300 days of sunshine a year.

The interior of the department is rich in vineyards, olive groves, lavender plantations, medieval towns, hilltop villages and market towns. The higher areas are popular ski resorts, but during the summer months they are fragranced by wild herbs and are popular with walkers. The city of Draguignan is set in the centre of Var and is famous for its Côte-de-Provence wine. The areas stretching from and around Adrets de l'Esterel, through Brignoles to Castellet, are prolific flower growers and produce fruit, vegetables, honey, lavender, thyme and olive oil.

The Mediterranean coastline, which is often seen as an extension of the Riviera that lies further east, boasts beautiful, sandy beaches, rocky inlets and picturesque islands, such as the Îles d'Hyères, whilst chic, partying St-Tropez hosts the *poseurs* and rich and famous with their yachts. So, along with the people-watching and sunbathing potential, Var has something for every taste, from the opera at Toulon to horseback riding and rock climbing in the centre of the department; from canoeing and kayaking on the Ste-Croix and St-Cassien lakes to diving and sailing in the Mediterranean Sea.

VINEYARDS
Le Castellet

Vineyards circle the pretty little feudal village of le Castellet, which is perched on a hillside above the plains of Var and is famous for its AOC Côte-de-Provence and AOC Bandol wines. The former fortified village still has some ancient ramparts and quaint cobbled streets. The red and orange of the wisteria, fuchsia and bougainvillea on the renovated stone walls of the village houses make le Castellet a very colourful village. Panoramic views of the vineyards and the Ste-Baume massif are exceptional from the fifteenth-century chateau in the village.

HARBOUR AND PROMENADE
Bandol

Bandol's port area is capable of sheltering up to 1,500 boats of all sizes, including great sailing boats and professional fishing boats and yachts. Bandol's cliffs, numerous beaches and small inlets, not to mention the Mediterranean climate, make it a popular family holiday destination and popular with scuba divers. The Bandol wine region is one of Provence's most famous, particularly for its rosé. The red wine of the region is especially noted for its dark colour and strong flavours of cinnamon and vanilla, as well as black fruits.

HARBOUR
Sanary-sur-Mer

This little fishing village and port was founded in the sixteenth century, under the name of Saint Nazari. It was granted independence from the commune of Ollioules in 1688, and its new name of Sanary-sur-Mer was officially formalized in 1923. There is a sixteenth-century Chapelle Notre-Dame-de-Pitié on a headland to the west from which panoramic views of the port can be had. There is also a late-nineteenth-century Gothic-revival church, which was built by Michel Pacha (1819–1907). The port has colourful facades, terraces shaded by palm trees and a daily flower market.

MARINA
Toulon

Toulon is a large city, with a busy international and military port and Mont Faron as its backdrop. It is the capital of the Var region and fulfills the role of French naval base for all of the Mediterranean; it is also a marina for private boats and ferries to Corsica and Sardinia. In the old town there are several small squares, narrow streets and fountains, as well as the Cathédrale Notre-Dame-de-la-Seds and the impressive Marché Provençal. Built in the mid-nineteenth century, the upper town hosts the Opéra, the place de la Liberté and the Jardin Alexandre Ier.

VILLAGE STREET
Fox-Amphoux

The sixteenth and seventeenth-century houses at the entrance to the village of Fox-Amphoux and the quaint little chapel of Notre-Dame du Bon Secours make this a very picturesque village. Fox-Amphoux is a Roman hilltop village, perched high above pine and oak forests and the main industry of the area is agriculture. There are several historic sites to visit for such a small village, including the preserved ruins of the ramparts of the Château des Blacas and a Roman temple. The house of a French revolutionary called Barras can also be visited.

VILLAGE AND ÉGLISE ST-DENIS
Tourtour

Officially classified as one of the prettiest villages in France, Tourtour overlooks a vast area of Provence. The church of St Denis, with its Roman architecture and view of the village, lies to the east and an old medieval castle lies to the west. The village was built in the eleventh century, but ramparts from the fourteenth and fifteenth centuries can also be seen near the present village square. Tourtour's springs – the principal of which is the Saint-Rosaire spring – supply the village's eight fountains, and there is also a water-powered mill still in use in the village.

TOWARDS THE VILLAGE
Villecroze

Villecroze, just south of Tourtour in the Haut Var, is surrounded by pines and oak trees and perched above a large group of caves, which now form part of a municipal park. Also in the park are rare trees, a waterfall and rose gardens. A vaulted passageway leads to the *vieille ville*, with its narrow streets, arcades, an old dungeon attached to its castle, an elegant campanile, a seventeenth-century church and the twelfth-century St-Victor chapel. A *commanderie* (Templar monastery) built in the mid-twelfth century by the Templiers du Ruou is located southeast of Villecroze.

VILLAGE AND RUINED TOWERS
Cotignac

The two ruined towers, or *sentinelles*, overlooking Cotignac from atop a high cliff full of cave dwellings carved into the rock, have been guarding the town since the twelfth and thirteenth centuries. The old quarter of the village is set next to the cliff and features narrow streets lined with sixteenth- and seventeenth-century houses, decorated in stone or wrought iron. There are many fountains in the village and the Cours – inspired by the Cours Mirabeau in Aix-en-Provence – is a favourite eating place, lined with shady plane trees and cooled by one of the fountains.

VILLAGE AND ÉGLISE ST-SAUVEUR
Entrecasteaux

Set in the green valley of Bresque, this eleventh-century village houses the fortified church of St Sauveur. The massive castle in the centre of the village was built in the sixteenth or seventeenth century on the ruins of a medieval castle. Perfectly restored, it was the home of a number of Provençal noblemen, and in the 1970s of the Scots painter Ian McGarvie-Munn, who added his own touch. It also has a garden designed by Le Nôtre. The village is very pretty, with its vaulted passageways, decorated lintels, tall and narrow facades, as well as a wash house and two bridges.

PRESQU'ÎLE DE GIENS
near Hyères

The area of Hyères includes the town itself, the seaside peninsular of Presqu'île de Giens and the islands of Porquerolles, Port-Cros and the Levant. Presqu'île de Giens has an old fortress, 'La Tour Fondue', that sits on a promontory jutting into the sea with ferry links to the other islands. At the centre of the peninsular is a village and the old castle, which dates to the reign of Louis IX and was built as a defence of the island after he returned from the crusades. The city of Hyères and the peninsular have nearly 40 km (25 miles) of fine, sandy beaches and rocky inlets.

CITY AND COLLÉGIALE ST-PAUL
Hyères

The Collégiale St-Paul, the church seen here, was listed as an historic monument in 1992. Classed as a middle-sized city, Hyères boasts a number of accolades, including 'the palm tree capital of Europe' and the 'Quatre Fleurs' label, representing its status as one of France's best 'towns in bloom'. Hyères' gardens provide many rare species of plant and superb views can be had from the Parc St-Bernard, which lies at the top of the old town. Above this is the Villa Noailles, which was designed in the 1920s by Robert Mallet-Stevens (1886–1945).

TOUR ST-BLAISE
Hyères

The fourteenth-century Porte Massillon gateway leads into the heart of the old town, to the place Massillon, where you can find this twelfth-century tower, which was once a command post of the Knights Templar. It has a rooftop terrace and provides panoramic views over Hyères. The city's Gothic church of St Louis, in the Place de la République, is thirteenth century and has Renaissance doorways, an 1878 organ, a beautiful stone retable, an 1846 marble Florentine Virgin and a seventeenth-century crucified Christ.

ÎLES D'HYÈRES
off the coast of Hyères

The Îles d'Hyères, or Golden Islands, are three islands that lie off the coast of Var. Made up of Île de Porquerolles, Île de Port-Cros and Île du Levant, they have been inhabited by various peoples over the centuries, including the Ligurians, the Greeks, the Romans and the Lerians. Île de Porquerolles, the largest island, is approximately four miles long, while Île de Port-Cros, the central of the three islands, is thickly forested and has a deep, hollowed out harbour. The Île du Levant is a long, rocky ridge with a fort built by Napoleon in 1812, and the town of Héliopolis, which is dedicated to naturism.

HARBOUR
Le Lavandou

Le Lavandou, formerly a small fishing port but now home to many more yachts than fishing boats, faces the 'Golden Islands' of Îles d'Hyères. Located in the Massif des Maures region of Var, le Lavandou is renowned for the quality of its numerous, sandy beaches such as la Fosette and at Aiguebelle, and the area is particularly popular with divers and snorkelers. The town's small Église St-Louis was built in 1855, and the 'castle', which has also been known as 'Villa Louise' and now houses municipal services, was finished in 1881 after forty years of construction.

VILLAGE STREET
Ramatuelle

Closed in by ramparts and built in the shape of a snail, the village of Ramatuelle has typically narrow streets, lined with ochre facades and houses beautifully adorned with pastel-coloured shutters, jasmine, honeysuckle and bougainvillea. The Romanesque parish church of Notre Dame sits against the ancient fortifications of the village. Built on the hillside, Ramatuelle offers magnificent views of the bay of Pampelonne and the famous beach of the same name, which is carved with inlets and stretches for 5 km (3 miles) alongside crystal-clear water.

LE MOULIN DE PAILLAS
near *Ramatuelle*

The windmills of Paillas (there were originally five) were built between the sixteenth and nineteenth centuries and named after Jean-Baptiste Paillas, who was the first miller of Ramatuelle. Most have disappeared or are in ruins, but one was restored in 2002 to how it would have been when it was built in the nineteenth century. Built in three parts: the base, the tower and the roof, it is typical of Provençal windmills in that the upper part rotates to catch the wind. Situated on the windy hilltop of Castellas, it affords a panoramic view over to St-Tropez.

BOATS DOCKED IN THE HARBOUR
St-Tropez

Since the 1950s, St-Tropez has been the playground of
chic Parisians and international jet-setters; its harbour
usually boasts a line of yachts of the rich and famous and its
peninsular is lined with forty beaches. Despite the glitz and
glamour, the town itself does have some charming streets
and fishermen who still go about their daily work, while
the Place Carnot is lined with cafés and occupied by games
of pétanque or fruit and vegetable markets. There is an
eighteenth-century church and bell tower and the locals
still maintain a fifteenth-century custom of processing
through the street with the bust of the patron saint (St
Torpes) in May.

PAMPELONNE BEACH
Baie de Pampelonne

With a long, sandy beach and bars, Pampelonne is very popular with visitors to the south of France. The beach stretches for 5 km (3 miles) from the peninsula of St-Tropez in the north to Cap Camarat in the south and consists of a group of twenty-seven public and private beaches. Originally used as a landing beach for fishing boats, Pampelonne became famous during the Second World War after the allied landings in Provence took place (first called 'Operation Anvil' but renamed 'Operation Dragoon'). Since then the beach has regularly been the haunt of the jet set.

VILLAGE AND ÉGLISE ST-MICHEL
Grimaud

This twelfth-century, Romanesque church has a distinctive, square clock tower. Overlooking the Golfe de St-Tropez, Grimaud is perched on a forested hillside in the Massif des Maures and is dominated by the striking ruins of an eleventh-century castle. Pretty, winding streets lined with newly renovated, traditional houses, lead up to the church of St Michel past several of Grimaud's old fountains. There is also a Chapelle des Pénitents, which dates from the fifteenth century, two other chapels and the seventeenth-century Moulin St-Roch just outside the village.

CHÂTEAU DE GRIMAUD
Grimauld

This castle with round corner towers and crenellated ramparts surrounding it stands proud over the village of Grimaud. Built during the eleventh century and rebuilt in the fifteenth century, the chateau was torn down by Richelieu (1585–1642) in the seventeenth century and partially rebuilt once more by Jean de Cossa. The castle still features underground passageways and the ramparts that remain are used as a backdrop for summer theatre shows. Grimaud is one of the richest towns in the Var region of Provence and produces wine, honey, flowers and chestnuts.

VILLAGE AND CASTLE KEEP
Les Arcs-sur-Argens

Les Arcs is a restored medieval village that perches on a hillside and boasts the remains of an eleventh-century castle. Wine made since the fourteenth century is produced from the vineyards surrounding the castle, which also has a dungeon and a chapel. Ste Roseline was born at the castle in 1263 and the Chapelle Ste-Roseline, at the Abbaye de la Celle-Roubaud outside the village, contains her relics. The old town has narrow, cobbled streets, arched doorways and vaulted passageways. Les Arcs also has a fortified clock tower topped with a campanile.

VILLAGE AND ÉGLISE ST-MICHEL
Ampus

The tiny tenth–century village of Ampus is perched high –
600 m (1,970 ft) – above sea level and has retained many
Roman and medieval features, including its church. Forming
the historical centre of the village, the church of St Michel
was built in the eleventh century, but was renovated and
enlarged during the eighteenth century. The village's streets
are arranged concentrically around the ruins of a castle,
which has an eleventh-century gateway and small squares.
There are panoramic views from Ampus village over the
surrounding countryside.

OVERLOOKING THE VILLAGE
Bargemon

At an altitude of 480 m (1,575 ft), Bargemon is surrounded by olive groves and close to the lakes of Ste Croix and St Cassien, as well as the Verdon canyons. The village itself has shady trees and cooling fountains and several historical buildings: the ramparts of the village retain their medieval gateways, such as La Porte de la Prison, part of the former gaol dating from 1582. The Église Ste-Etienne and the seventeenth-century Chapelle Notre-Dame de Montaigu can also be visited, along with the Musée Camos in the old Chapelle Ste-Etienne, near the cemetery.

VILLAGE AND CHATEAU
Trigance

The chateau perched on a rocky outcrop is the first sight as the village of Trigance is approached by car. This fortified monastery was built by the monks of St-Victor abbey most probably around the ninth century. The beautiful medieval village full of ancient houses, vaulted passageways, decorated lintels and stepped streets snuggles into the hillside at the foot of the castle. Sitting in the Jabron Valley, on the doorstep of the canyons of Verdon, Trigance is popular with bird-watchers in search of buzzards, golden eagles and hawks.

TOWARDS THE VILLAGE
Seillans

Classified as 'one of the most beautiful villages in France', Seillans dates back to 500 BC and is nestled into a forested mountain backdrop. Full of ancient buildings, narrow, cobbled streets and tree-shaded squares, Seillans has a Saracen door and a number of fountains. The village centre is only accessible by foot and has a feudal castle and an eleventh-century church. The twelfth-century Chapelle Notre-Dame de l'Ormeau is 2 km (1¼ miles) outside the village. Seillans' houses are painted the colour of ochre and rise above one another from the bottom of the village to the top.

BAPTISTERY OF
CATHÉDRALE ST-LÉONCE
Fréjus

The baptistery of this Roman Catholic cathedral was built in the fifth century and is the oldest Christian structure in Provence, while the cathedral cloister is a national monument of France. Fréjus is an ancient military port between Cannes and St-Tropez; Julius Caesar founded the city in 49 BC and it still remains an import harbour. Historic buildings include Roman ruins, an amphitheatre and a large aqueduct. In 1959 the city experienced fatalities when the Malpasset Dam broke and flooded the western part of Fréjus.

MASSIF DE L'ESTEREL

eastern Var coast

This protected coastal mountain range is volcanic in origin, with rugged terrain, deep ravines and former forests of oak trees, which have been devastated by forest fires. Stretching for 39 km (24 miles) along the coast from St Raphael to la Napoule, it rises to 618 m (2,028 ft) at its peak, Mont Vinaigre. The volcanic rock is predominantly made of porphyry, which gives the landscape the red colour. Full of numerous caves, this terrain was the former stamping ground of the highwayman Gaspard de Besse, who was caught and hanged in Aix-en-Provence.

ALPES DE HAUTE-PROVENCE

This wild, mountainous, lake-filled region of Provence has eleven villages that have been classified as having special architectural character.

The Alpes de Haute-Provence department lies at the heart of the larger region known as Provence-Alpes-Côte-d'Azur and incorporates alpine valleys and peaks, heady mountain passes and nationally protected areas of natural heritage. In the north are the mountains that form the valley of Ubaye and the Parc National du Mercantour (which mostly lies in Alpes-Maritimes), with the highest peaks and most dramatic scenery of the region. Further south, the Plateau de Valensole, with its fields of lavender, thyme and almond trees is differently but equally beautiful.

The southern border with the department of Var is partially marked by the River Verdon, and here are the famous Gorges (or Grand Canyon) of Verdon, rich in flora and fauna, with breathtaking scenery and the lakes of Ste Croix, Quinson and Esparron de Verdon. Alpes de Haute-Provence is an area of huge contrasts and of villages and towns rich in military, religious and natural history. Typical of the area are villages specializing in faience pottery and lavender distilleries, to say nothing of the culinary delights of mushrooms, lamb, goats' cheese and nougat that are enjoyed in shady squares, accompanied by the bubbling of a fountain.

TOWARDS THE VILLAGE
Colmars-les-Alpes

This superb alpine village in the Alpes de Haute-Provence is surrounded by magnificent wooded mountains. The village also has an interesting history and military heritage. It is enclosed in ringed ramparts, dating originally from the fourteenth century, but developed from the seventeenth century with the addition of two forts. Colmars-les-Alpes is a quaint village, with narrow streets and squares with pretty fountains. It is also close to the northern part of Parc National du Mercantour and in wintertime it is a useful base for skiing enthusiasts.

FORT DE FRANCE
Colmars-les-Alpes

The Fort de France lies to the south of Colmars-les-Alpes, in the Verdon Valley. Its sister, the much larger Fort de Savoie, lies to the north. Both forts were built strategically when France was at war with Savoie. In the French Wars of Religion, Colmars-les-Alpes was the target of several attacks. In 1560 the village came under attack from Paulon de Mauvans and again in 1582 Captain Cartier ransomed the village. A few years later the French Catholic League sacked Colmars-les-Alpes. A fortified path leads down from the Fort de France to the Porte de France.

TOWARDS THE VILLAGE
Lurs

Set on high, overlooking the Durance Valley, the village houses in Lurs appear to be built on top of one another. With a clock tower, boasting one of the oldest clocks in Provence and a wrought-iron belfry, at the entrance to the fortfied village and a narrow maze of streets, Lurs is an attractive town. It was inhabited by the bishops of Sisteron during the ninth century, who built a chateau and a seminary there. To the north of the village can be seen the monastery of Ganagobie, founded by the bishops of Sisteron in the tenth century.

NOTRE-DAME-DE-VIE

Lurs

The fourteenth-century chapel of Notre-Dame-de-Vie in
Lurs was restored in 1995 by The Friends of Lurs Association
and lies at the end of the Promenade des Évêques, a ridgeway
path lined with shrines. The whole village of Lurs is steeped
in history and it is believed that no fewer than seventy-six
bishops of Sisteron lived there through the centuries. The
village still retains several other historical monuments from a
variety of eras, including the St-Michel chapel at the
entrance to the village.

TOWARDS THE VILLAGE
Annot

This pretty, eleventh-century village in the Vaire valley is surrounded by wooded hills and is located between the Parc National du Mercantour and the Gorges du Verdon. It is built predominantly from sandstone, and large rocks of it are visible in the surrounding countryside. The cobbled labyrinth of streets is lined with old stone houses and beautifully decorated gateways, revealing colourful Mediterranean-style gardens. The village has an old wash house and some pretty little tree-shaded squares with fountains.

BRIDGE OVER THE RIVER VAIRE
Annot

The River Vaire runs through the centre of Annot, under this four-arched seventeenth-century stone bridge which connects the old part of the town with the newer section. The town is surrounded by the distinctive Grès d'Annot, the sandstone cliffs that have been popular with both painters and hikers for many years, and is one of many towns and villages on the route of the Train des Pignes. This popular scenic train route travels between Nice and Digne-les-Bains four times daily, and a steam train operates on weekends between May and October.

TOWARDS THE VILLAGE
Méailles

The picturesque, old village of Méailles is laid out in a strip on the edge of a rocky plateau 325 m (1,070 ft) above the River Vaire. The village is surrounded by farms and farm animals and this is very much still the main occupation of the residents. With narrow, winding village roads the streets are full of interesting nooks and crannies to explore. Many of the beige stone houses in this serene village have been restored to their former glory, with roofs clad with Roman tiles of black, red and green and dark wood doors and window frames.

STEPS IN THE VILLAGE
Méailles

Steps constructed from sandstone are common in the village of Méailles, which has vaulted passageways lying beneath its medieval houses. The area from Annot to Méailles is littered with huge, sandstone boulders. A couple of miles away are the Grottes de Méailles, limestone caves with beautiful stalactites and crystal-clear pools of water. The caves are thought to be dated to the Bronze Age and certainly the tools and pottery found in the caves of Méailles and St Benoît prove that they were occupied by ancient peoples.

CHURCH
Méailles

The view of Méailles from the steep, winding road leading into the village is dominated by the striking square bell tower on the beautiful fourteenth- and fifteenth-century church, with its slated roof. It is built from dressed stone in the colour of the region, pale beige sandstone, and the Latin inscription on the church's sundial reads 'Fugit Irreparabile Tempus', mourning the irrepressible passage of time. Inside the church there is a magnificent altarpiece listed as sixteenth-century, and also two paintings, called the *Déposition de la Croix* and the *Donation du Rosaire*.

TOWN AND CITADEL
Entrevaux

Listed as one of the one thousand most beautiful villages of France, the walled town of Entrevaux was fortified by Vauban (1633–1707) in 1690 on the orders of Louis XIV (1638–1715), in his efforts to defend France from the Savoie. With zigzagging ramps leading to a seventeenth-century citadel, tall, narrow houses and small public squares, Entrevaux has retained much of its historical and military architecture. The old town radiates a medieval feel and has a high drawbridge entrance through a vaulted gate between two towers.

CATHÉDRALE
NOTRE-DAME-DE L'ASSOMPTION
Entrevaux

During the sixteenth century, the original Glandèves cathedral was abandoned as the official bishop's seat and a new cathedral, dedicated to the Virgin Mary, was constructed in Entrevaux. The Gothic and baroque Notre-Dame-de l'Assomption has the only crenellated bell tower in Provence, a portal crowned with a statue of the Virgin and a stunning gold-leaf alterpiece. The cathedral became the formal seat of the diocese in the seventeenth century, and is known as both Entrevaux Cathedral and Glandèves Cathedral.

TOWN AND CHURCH
Moustiers-Ste-Marie

Located in the Grand Canyon du Verdon, Moustiers-Ste-Marie is renowned for its earthenware tiles and pottery, especially faience. At 630 m (2,060 ft) altitude, the village is set on rocky cliffs above the gorge of the Rioul torrent, across which runs an iron chain sporting the star of Blacas, one of the knights of the Crusades. The twelfth-century church in the centre, seen here, is dominated by its three-tiered Romanesque bell tower. Moustiers-Ste-Marie has interesting paths meandering through the town and narrow alleyways, tiny squares and fountains.

RAVIN DE NOTRE DAME
above Moustiers-Ste-Marie

Led to by a magnificent series of steps, the Ravin de Notre
Dame gushes above the town of Moustiers-Ste-Marie. In
this setting is the Chapelle Notre-Dame de Beauvoir. Built
in the twelfth century, this chapel is still a pilgrimage site.
Decorated with fine faience, produced for centuries in
Moustiers-Ste-Marie, the chapel was built high up on the
rock face and the surrounding caves were inhabited by
monks for many years. Remodelled in the sixteenth century,
the porch of the chapel gives a superb view of the town's
red-tiled roofs and the green valley with its olive groves.

LAVENDER
Plateau de Valensole

In the summer months the aromas on the Plateau de Valensole
mingle with the sunshine to give a rich smell of lavender and
thyme. This is one of the main and most famous lavender-
producing areas and some of the distilleries still use traditional
methods in processing the flowers. The 'Valley of the Sun' also
grows almond trees and the town of Valensole itself has an
eleventh-century church, the fourteenth-century church of
St Blaise with its richly decorated interior, seventeenth- and
eighteenth-century renovated houses, ramparts, fountains,
wash houses and chapels.

RIEZ
Plateau de Valensole

Riez is situated in the wide, rich valley of Colostre, in the centre of the Plateau de Valensole, and the surrounding countryside is full of lavender fields. Dating to the first century, its ancient heritage is evidenced by the baptistery and remains of the cathedral, both from the fifth century. The village also has two fourteenth-century rampart gates: the eastern one, the Porte Aiguière, has the remains of a *lavoir* (a stone building used for washing) and a fountain, smaller versions of which are at the western porte, the Porte St-Sol.

CHAPELLE STE-MAXIME
near Riez

Riez is dominated by the Colline Ste-Maxime, which
currently houses a park but was a former hilltop capital.
Perched on a cedar-shaded platform on the hill, the only
building remaining on the site, is the seventeenth-century
Chapelle Ste-Maxime, which is now inhabited by nuns. Both
the chapel and the ridge of Colline Ste-Maxime offer
commanding and spectacular views of the surrounding
countryside and the Valley of Colostre. Riez is a medieval and
Renaissance city, also with the remains of a Roman temple.

CHAPELLE STE-MAXIME INTERIOR
near Riez

The interior of the Chapelle Ste-Maxime is brightly and intricately (some would say gaudily) patterned. Back down the hill from the chapel, from the ground below the oak trees on the Ste-Maxime ridge, truffles are often harvested. In addition to these and the many other aromatic products of the area, honey-making is celebrated at the Maison de l'Abeille, nearby on the road to Digne. Here you can learn all about old-fashioned honey production, the life cycle of the bee and beekeeping, and finish it off with a purchase of lavender honey in the shop.

GRAND CANYON DU VERDON
between Casellane and Moustiers-Ste-Marie

Considered to be Europe's most beautiful gorge, the Grand Canyon (or Gorges) du Verdon is the second largest in the world. The river has sliced through the limestone rock in some areas to a depth of 700 m (2,295 ft), providing incredible views from atop the sheer cliffs. One of the canyon's most impressive features is the River Verdon itself, which ranges from a brilliant and bright emerald green to turquoise blue. At the end of the canyon the Verdon flows into the 10-km (6¼-mile) long artificial lake, Lac de Ste-Croix, surrounded by the Haut-Var hills and the Plateau de Valensole.

ALPES-MARITIMES

The department of Alpes-Maritimes includes the famous 70-km (44-mile) long stretch of Mediterranean coastline of the Côte d'Azur, also known as the French Riviera.

Known for its beaches, the Cannes Film Festival, the city of Nice and the Alps (the western part of the range, specifically the Maritime Alps), the region is mountainous right down to the seashore – the craggy landscape drops down into the Mediterranean Sea in spectacular fashion in places. The coastline is dotted with old fishing ports, palatial houses and luxury villas all the way to the Italian border.

The inland section of this department is very different; as the roads begin to climb and twist into the mountains, the aroma of pines, thyme and olive trees attack the senses. The scenery incorporates giant cacti and flowering laurel and the constant singing of the cicadas in the hot sun remind you that you are definitely in the *south* of France. High in the Alps are the snow-capped peaks and quaint, medieval villages scattered here and there, often in quite precarious positions, perched on rocky ridges or nestled in valleys. This region offers fabulous skiing, canoeing and kayaking for enthusiasts, in addition to the hiking and walking opportunities.

LAKE TRECOLPAS AREA
Parc National du Mercantour

This national park begins in Alpes de Haute-Provence (see pages 120–43) but mostly lies in Alpes-Maritimes. Some of the peaks in this mountainous area exceed 3,000 m (9,900 ft) and are surrounded by a varied landscape of pastureland, forests, lakes and canyons and over 2,000 plant species, including lilies and orchids. The area runs for over 128 km (80 miles) from Barcelonnette, in Alpes de Haute-Provence, to Sospel, and is home to many birds of prey and colonies of chamois and ibex. In the Vallée des Merveilles the park also boasts Bronze-Age rock engravings.

LA CROISETTE
Cannes

A former small fishing village, Cannes has become an elegant, international city, famous for the Cannes Film Festival. Created during the nineteenth century, this 3-km (1¾-mile) long promenade, which hugs the seashore and its beaches, is one of the most famous in the world. La Croisette is host to colourful flowering gardens, opulent hotels, palm trees within luscious green lawns and play parks for children. Named after the small cross that formerly stood to the east of the bay, views from the promenade of the Îles de Lerins and the Massif de l'Esterel provide stunning scenery.

SKYLINE FROM HARBOUR SQUARE
Cannes

Along Canne's Quai St-Pierre in the Vieux Port, fishing boats, expensive yachts and tourist boats bob, but the view up to the haute ville, le Suquet, on the skyline, reveals the city's much older heritage. Perched on Mont Chevalier are the keep, Romanesque Ste-Anne chapel and cisterns of the medieval castle, which was used as a retreat by the monks from Îles de Lérins, along with the seventeenth-century late-Gothic Église Notre-Dame d'Espérance. The stunning views from here include the islands of Ste-Marguerite and Ste-Honorat in the near distance.

PALAIS DES FESTIVALS
Cannes

Situated on the eastern side of the old port of Cannes,
on the Esplanade Georges Pompidou, is the Palais des Festivals
et des Congrès, the home of the Cannes International Film
Festival. This large and impressive building is capable of
housing many kinds of events as well as cinema, including
conventions, conferences, concerts, dance and theatre. The
building also houses four casinos. Replacing the former Palais
des Festivals on the Boulevard de la Croisette – which was
rechristened 'Palais Croisette' and demolished in 1988 – the
current structure was completed in 1982 and hosted its first
film festival in 1983.

HARBOUR AND FORT CARRÉ
Antibes

Although Antibes is a small town, it has a history as an important trading centre and a stormy past because of its much desired strategic position. Set atop a rock 26 m (85 ft) above sea level, the Fort Carré is a star-shaped fortress of four corners – hence 'squared fort' – surrounded by protected natural parkland. Built on a site of previous ancient Greek and Roman occupancy, in the second half of the sixteenth century on the orders of Henri II (1519–59), it was improved and extended at the end of the seventeenth century by Vauban, who also fortified Antibes itself by erecting bastions.

VILLAGE STREET
Haut-de-Cagnes

Of medieval origin, this village in the Cagnes-sur-Mer district in Alpes-Maritimes has a reputation for being a photographer's haven. Nestled around a castle once owned by the Grimaldi dynasty, Haut-de-Cagnes commands uninterrupted, panoramic views of the Var valley and the Mediterranean Sea from Nice to Antibes. Some of the houses in the village date back to the fourteenth century and many have been tastefully restored. The Château Grimaldi houses a part of the collection of portraits of the thirties Parisian singer, Suzy Solidor, who was painted some 150 times.

ST-PAUL-DE-VENCE
north of Cagnes-sur-Mer

St-Paul-de-Vence (then simply 'St Paul') was founded in the
ninth century. The chateau of St Paul dominated the village for
many years; but now the only surviving part of the castle today
is its dungeon. With many listed buildings, the village boasts a
raft of relics from the past, including ramparts, a square-bell-
towered church, one of the most famous fountains in France (la
Grande Fontaine), a tiny covered bridge dating from the
fifteenth century and the Chapelle de Notre-Dame de la
Gardette, which was restored in the eighteenth century. Also, an
important art collection is housed in the Fondation Maeght.

FRUIT MARKET
St-Paul-de-Vence

With fruit and vegetable markets, not to mention flowers in
abundance, on the streets of St-Paul-de-Vence on most days,
it is not surprising that the gastronomy of this village centres
round fresh produce. St-Paul-de-Vence also has a strong
reputation for wine production. The approaches to this hilltop
village are lined with terraced vineyards of Mourvèdre, Braquet
and Clairette grape varieties and a fourteenth-century cellar
offers wine tasting sessions of village wine and those from
other areas of Provence. Vineyards have been in existence here
since the sixth century.

PROMENADE DES ANGLAIS
Nice

This well-known French Riviera resort is a major tourist centre and the former capital city of the historical 'County of Nice'. The famous Promenade des Anglais is so named because of the city's popularity as a winter retreat with the English since the eighteenth century. Two minutes inland from the promenade, the Place de Messéna is the main square in Nice, bordered with red, ochre belle époque buildings. The square is used for concerts, parades and Bastille Day processions. Other squares of interest are Place Garibaldi, Place Rosetti, Cours Saleya and Place Palais.

HÔTEL NEGRESCO
Nice

PORT AREA
Nice

This palatial hotel was named for the Romanian Henri Negresco (1868–1920), who built it in the early twentieth century. Although designed by architect Édouard Niemans, its famous pink dome was created by Gustave Eiffel (1832–1923). The hotel boasts a spectacular Baccarat crystal chandelier, containing 16,309 crystals. This was reputedly commissioned by Czar Nicholas II (1868–1918). With 119 guest rooms and twenty-two suites, the Hotel Negresco is now a National Historic Building and one of the Leading Hotels of the World and is famous for its doormen dressed in eighteenth-century elite bourgeois style.

The port area of Nice is linked to the old town and modern centre via the Place Garibaldi, behind the chateau and Quai Rauba Capeu, at the front. The harbour wall points out towards Cap Ferrat. The Place Île de Beauté lies at the heart of the port, with the Notre-Dame du Port church prominent among the neo-classical buildings. The view from the port incorporates the Colline du Château, which is now pleasant gardens with only the crumbling remains of the castle. The port, also known as Lympia Port, has ferry connections to Corsica.

CATHÉDRALE ORTHODOXE RUSSE
Nice

The Russian Royals used to visit Nice and the French Riviera
for the healthy sun and sea air. The original, smaller Cathédrale
Orthodoxe Russe St-Nicolas and Ste-Alexandra was built in
1858 on rue Longchamp, financed by the dowager empress
Alexandra Feodorovna, but it soon proved too small and the
first stone of the current structure was laid in 1903. It is the
largest building dedicated to Russian Orthodox religion outside
of Russia, with its domes, vivid colours and gilding. The
interior has many carved arches and liturgies and houses the
mausoleum of the Tsarevich Nicholas Alexandrovich, who died
of tubercolis in Nice in 1865.

BAY VIEW
Villefranche-sur-Mer

One of the deepest natural harbours in the Mediterranean
Sea, Villefranche-sur-Mer has a 500-m (1,650-ft) abyss off
the coastline, known as the undersea Canyon of Villefranche.
The hills surrounding the bay reach an altitude of 520 m
(1,700 ft) at Mont-Leuze and the old town is built on a
terrace overlooking the sea. Its labyrinth of streets boast
the sixteenth-century, walled Citadelle St-Elme and the
fourteenth-century Chapelle St-Pierre, decorated by
Jean Cocteau (1889–1963) among other sights. The
panoramic views from the Fort du Mont Alban extend
from Cap Ferrat to Italy.

VILLA EPHRUSSI DE ROTHSCHILD
Cap Ferrat

Béatrice Ephrussi de Rothschild (1864–1934), the wife of the wealthy banker Maurice Ephrussi (1849–1916), built this villa on Cap Ferrat, inspired by the great Renaissance palaces of Venice and Florence. The fanciful Beatrice chose pink as the dominant colour and filled the palatial residence with monkeys, budgerigars, mongooses, gazelles, antelopes and flamingos, as well as an extensive art collection. On her death in 1934 the villa was bequeathed to the Académie des Beaux Arts. Overlooking the bay of Villefranche-sur-Mer, the villa also houses fine eighteenth-century furniture and furnishings.

JARDIN D'ÈZE
Èze

Èze is the highest village perché in Provence at 430 m (1,410 ft) above sea level. At the very top, the garden (formerly known as the 'Jardin Exotique') surrounds the ruins of Èze's chateau, which was torn down in 1706 on the orders of Louis XIV. First opened in 1933, the garden exhibits a wide variety of cacti and succulent plants originating in the Americas, Africa and the Arab peninsular. From its high vantage point you can see the Chapelle des Pénitents Blancs between the roofs of the village, and the sweeping panorama of the coast from Italy to St-Tropez.

ARCHED DOORWAY
Èze

This old arched doorway near the Château de la Chèvre d'Or restaurant echoes the fourteenth-century Poterne, the main entrance to the winding streets of the eagle's nest village of Èze. This picturesque, cliff top village is steeped in history, while its surrounding lush tropical vegetation, including banana, date, carob, orange and lemon trees are testimony of the year-round warm climate. Narrow streets, archways, restored stone houses, shady squares and refreshing ancient fountains all combine to make this village one of the most popular with visitors to the region.

PORT DE FONTVIEILLE
Fontvieille, Monaco

Lying at the eastern end of the Côte d'Azur, between Cap d'Ail and Cap Martin, the principality of Monaco is a famous resort, popular with tourists and wealthy forigners, and a tax haven for businesses. The state has two ports, Port Hercule and the Port de Fontvieille. The larger Port Hercule is a natural, deep-water bay and can accommodate hundreds of vessels, some of which are extremely large and elegant, as well as cruise ships. Port de Fontvieille, bordering the newer quarter of Fontvieille, is smaller but much better protected from winds and swells.

PALAIS PRINCIER
Monaco-Ville, Monaco

Built on the site of a thirteenth-century Genoese fortress, the ornate Palais Princier overlooks the Place du Palais. Built and added to from the fourteenth to the eighteenth centuries, it boasts a range of styles, with an Italian-style gallery and frescoes by sixteenth-century Genoese artists, a yellow and gold Louis XV salon and a Mazarin salon with arabesque motifs. The throne room has a large Renaissance fireplace and the main courtyard, the Cour d'Honneur, is paved with several million white and coloured pebbles and has a magnificent staircase built in Carrara marble.

MONACO CATHEDRAL
Monaco-Ville, Monaco

Set in the heart of the old town, this cathedral was built in 1875
from white stone from La Turbie and stands on the site of a
thirteenth-century church dedicated to St Nicolas. It is the resting
place of the former princes, and the beloved Princess Grace
(1929–82), of Monaco, and houses a Great Altar and an Episcopal
throne in white marble from Carrara, an altarpiece painted by
Louis Bréa of Nice (1450–1523), *c*. 1500, and a magnificent four-
keyboard organ that was inaugurated in 1976. The immaculate
old town is also home to the Musée Océanographique, founded
in 1910 and built straight into the cliff face.

CASINO DE MONTE CARLO
Monte Carlo, Monaco

The Casino de Monte Carlo was built in 1878 by the architect
Charles Garnier (1825–98), who also designed the original Paris
Opéra. The auditorium of the Casino's opera, called the Salle
Garnier, is decorated in red and gold, with frescoes, sculptures
and bas reliefs. The atrium, which leads on to the Salle Garnier,
is paved in marble and surrounded by ionic columns built from
onyx. Each of the casino's successive number of gaming rooms,
such as the American Room and the European Room, are
decorated with sculptures, paintings, bronze lamps, stained glass
windows and impressive gilded rococo ceilings.

TOWARDS THE FRONT
Menton

The seafront of sunny Menton stretches from the old port, protected by La Bastion, to the newer port of Garavan nestled to the east, on the border with Italy. The harbour is dominated by the bell tower of the baroque Basilique St-Michel Archange, built between 1640 and the nineteenth century, when the facade was renovated and smooth columns with ionic and Corinthian capitals were added. The building was proclaimed a basilica in 1999 by Pope Jean-Paul II (1920–2005). Menton also boasts glorious gardens that flourish in the warm microclimate.

TOWARDS THE VILLAGE
Peillon

Less than 20 km (12½ miles) from Nice, the old fortified village of Peillon appears to cling, limpet-like, to the cliffs, in a spectacular setting high above the Paillon de l'Escarène valley. The tall, stone houses with ochre facades, the narrow, winding streets, wide stairs and vaulted passageways all contribute to the medieval air of the village. Picturesque and pedestrian-only, Peillon is considered one of the most beautiful perched villages in the Côte d'Azur region. It was originally part of the fief of Peille until 1235, when it separated from its twin and neighbour.

ÉGLISE ST-SAUVEUR DE LA TRANSFIGURATION
Peillon

The dignified parish church of Peillon, the sixteenth-century Église St-Sauveur de la Transfiguration, is built in a simple, rustic baroque style. It sits in the plaça de la Gleia on the site of an earlier twelfth-century church, and was itself added to and extended right up until the nineteenth century. Peillon also has a fifteenth-century Chapelle des Pénitents Blancs with a cycle of frescoes representing the passion of Christ, painted by Giovanni Canavesio (fl. late fifthteenth century) in 1495. In the centre of Peillon, on the tree-shaded Place Auguste-Arnulf, there is a fountain dating from around 1800.

VILLAGE AND ÉGLISE STE-MARGUERITE
Luceram

The medieval-ancient town of Luceram sits on top of a narrow ridge between two gorges, the buildings perched high on the rocks on either side of the deep ravine, with terraced gardens on the steep hills. The town's clock tower is on the Ste-Marguerite church, famous in the region for its Canavesio and Bréa altarpieces and treasure trove of religious silver and gold plate. Defensive remains include three fortified doors and an 'open-throated' guard tower and ramparts, built at the end of the fourteenth century, when the threat of Savoie accelerated the need for protection.

CHAPELLE ST-JEAN
Luceram

Luceram boasts three churches, one of which, the Chapelle St-Jean, houses the Musée des Vieux Outils et de L'Histoire Locale. This area has many chapels and sanctuaries that are part of the legends of the pilgrims of this area. On la Placette is the Le Musée de la Crèche, which houses over a hundred different crèches, traditionally nativity manger scenes but often elaborate models such as an intricate Provençal crèche that depicts medieval Luceram. Every year, in December and January, the village is filled with crèches of all shapes and sizes, on the Circuit des Crèches.

TOWARDS THE VALLEY
from Luceram

Luceram is surrounded by a varied landscape filled with rich
and diverse flora and fauna. The valleys and hills are terraced
with olive plantations, while higher up are chestnut forests and,
higher still, firs and larch. The town's setting means that the
narrow and steep streets are more like stairways and many of the
buildings are stacked one on top of the other, some being up to
six stories high and topped with open air attic rooms, said to be
for the drying of figs. From nearby Peïra Cava, a hamlet above
the village, the Sentier Botanique reveals the wide range of
mountain flowers and plants that can be seen.

SAORGE
La Roya Valley

The once-fortified stronghold village of Saorge was considered
to be impregnable, but its defences were finally destroyed at the
end of the eighteenth century. Overlooking the La Roya Valley,
the village is spread out across a narrow ridge above the river.
Previously known as 'La Roc de la Roya', it is one of the forty
'most beautiful villages of France'. The village streets are on
different levels and many of the houses are multi-storied. From
the village the panoramic views across the mountains, the gorge
and the river below are spectacular.

STONE BUILDING
Saorge

Lining the long, cobbled streets that lead to the monastery, the Couvent Franciscain, above the village of Saorge are its stone houses. Dating from between the fifteenth and seventeenth centuries, they are high and narrow – up to five stories high. Some are ochre with dark, red-purple slate roofs and others are constructed from blue stone. Others have picturesque details, like lintels, vaulted porches, murals, friezes and sundials. Once at the monastery the view across the village roofs and bell towers is superb.

COUVENT FRANCISCAIN
Saorge

This colourful Franciscan monastery sits high above the village of Saorge at its eastern end. Begun in 1661, all its buildings date to the seventeenth century, but it unfortunately suffered badly in the Second World War and is now restored. With trompe-l'oeil decorations on the facade, the interior has impressive woodwork and the cloister area is decorated with frescoes that represent the life of St Francis of Assisi. The view from the monastery sweeps across the village roofs and white facades of the tall houses and the bell tower of the Chapelle de la Madone del Poggio.

CHAPELLE DE LA MADONE DEL POGGIO
Saorge

Located down a steep slope below the village, on a spur to the southeastern edge of Saorge overlooking the Roya Valley, is the Chapelle de la Madone del Poggio. The eleventh-century sanctuary is Romanesque in design, with a 30-m (100-ft) high, Lombardy-style bell tower. Although the building has been restored, the interior is not open to the public. Other religious sites in Saorge include the Église St-Sauveur and three Chapelles des Pénitents with glazed bell towers, which were built in the seventeenth century and owned by the humanitarian brotherhoods.

LA BRIGUE
Levenza Valley

Nestling at the foot of the Massif Marguareis mountains, at 800 m (2,600 ft) altitude, with the Levenza river flowing past, this enchanting village has cobbled streets, archways and brightly coloured and decorated houses, many of which are built from local green schist. Some of La Brigue's houses have sculpted door lintels, often with the image of the lamb, representing the village's long pastoral tradition, and there are also many niches – little alcove shrines to the Virgin – dotted throughout. La Brigue celebrates its historic past with a La Fête Médiévale every summer.

COLLÉGIALE ST-MARTIN
La Brigue

Classified as an historic monument, the collegiate church of St Martin with its Gothic bell tower was rebuilt in Romanesque style during the fifteenth century using the ruins of the old thirteenth-century building. It has an unusual striped facade and important pictures attributed to Louis Bréa adorn the interior, including *The Nativity*. Located near the church are the Chapelle de l'Annonciation, which has a monumental baroque facade, and the unusual octagonal Chapelle St-Michel situated on the Place de Nice.

CHÂTEAU DES LASCARIS WATCHTOWER
La Brigue

All that remains of the fourteenth-century Château des Lascaris is the tall, round donjon or watchtower. The chateau was the first residence of Count Ludovic Lascaris, lord of half of Limone and first lord of la Brigue in 1376, but it is not known how long it remained in use, watching over the village and at some point it was abandoned and left to slide into ruins over the centuries. It is known, however, that it was used as a watchtower by the Germans in the Second World War. The first urgent restoration works were carried out in 1993 to conserve this rare tower.

CHAPELLE NOTRE-DAME DE FONTAINES
La Brigue

The Chapelle Notre-Dame de Fontaines is situated about 4 km (2½ miles) to the east of La Brigue and has been a major pilgrimage site for many years. Reached by a winding road that crosses a delightful zigzag bridge, the Pont du Coq, and set beside a mountain stream on a small cleared site in a thickly forested area, the setting is idyllic and very tranquil. The chapel appears in records as early as 1375 and, according to legend, its construction and site was decided when, the springs of La Brigue having dried up, the inhabitants prayed to the Virgin and the water miraculously returned.

INTERIOR OF THE CHAPELLE NOTRE-DAME DE FONTAINES
La Brigue

This pretty little chapel boasts a series of frescoes on the triumphal arch and the walls of the nave attributed to Giovanni Canavesio, which were completed in 1492. The arch bears eleven panels, illustrating the life of the Virgin and Christ's childhood. On the lateral walls are twenty-six panels, which illustrate the cycle of the Passion, with the Crucifixion occupying the whole height of the wall. On the western wall of the chapel is Canavesio's monumental, 4-m (12-ft) high, *Last Judgement*. The choir area with its Gothic vaults was painted by Jean Baleison around 1460.

INDEX

Abbaye-de-Sénanque *30*, 31
Adrets de l'Esterel 87
Aix-en-Provence 6, 8, 47, 49,71, 72–75,
    77, 95, 119
    Aquae Sextiae 73
    Cathédrale St-Sauveur 73, *73*
    Cours Mirabeau 75, 95
    fountains *74*, 75
    Tour de l'Horloge *72*, 73
    Tourreluquo Tower 73
Agrippa, Marcus Vipsanius 59
Aigues-Mortes 62
    Église Notre-Dame-des-Sablons 62
    ramparts 62, *63*
    Tour de Constance 62
Alpes de Haute-Provence 7, 14,
    120–43, 146
Alpes-Maritimes & Côte d'Azur 7,
    144–89
Alpilles mountains 49, 51, 53, 54, *55*
Alps 7, 8, 11, 145
Ampus *112*, 113
    castle 113
    Église St-Michel *112*, 113
Annot *128*, 129, 131
    Grès d'Annot 129
Ansouis 46–47
    Château d'Anouis *46*, 47
    Église St-Martin 47, *47*
Antibes 152, *152*
    Fort Carré 152, *152*
Apt 11, 42, *43*, 47
Les Arcs-sur-Argens 111, *111*
    Abbaye de la Celle-Roubaud 111
    Chapelle Ste-Roseline 111
Arles 7, 49, 62
    Les Arènes 62, *62*
Augustus, Emperor 59
Aurel 14, *15*
Avignon 6, 8, 9, 27–29, 61
    chapel of St Nicholas 27
    Palais des Papes 6, 11, *28*, 29
    Pont St-Bénezét 27, *27*

Bandol 87, 88, *89*
Barcelonette 146
Bargemon *114*, 115

La Porte de la Prison 115
Barras, Paul François Jean Nicolas 93
Les Baux-de-Provence 51–53, 62
    Château des Baux *52*, 53
    Église St-Vincent 51, *51*
Beaumes de Venise 6
Bonnieux 38, 40–42
    Musée de la Boulangerie 40
    Neuve Église 40, *41*
    Pont Julien bridge 11, 42, *42*
    bories 34
Bouches-du-Rhône 6, 8, 48–85
Bresque 96
Brignoles 87
La Brigue 184–89
    Chapelle de l'Annonciation 185
    Chapelle St-Michel 185
    Chapelle Notre-Dame de Fontaines
        188, 189, *189*
    Château des Lascaris watchtower
        186, 187
    Collégiale St-Martin 185, *185*
    Pont du Coq 189
bullfighting 7, 56, 62, 65

Cagnes-sur-Mer 152, 155
Les Calanques 49, 81, *81*, 85
Camargue 7, 8, 49, 64–67
    bulls 7, 49, 65, *65*
    flamingos 7, 49, *66*, 67
    horses 7, 49, *64*, 65
Canaille, Cap *84*, 85
Cannes 7, 117, 148–51
    castle 148
    La Croisette 148, *148*
    Église Notre-Dame d'Espérance 148
    Esplanade Georges Pompidou 151
    Film Festival 145, 148, 151
    Palais des Festivals *150*, 151
    Ste-Anne chapel 148
    Le Suquet 148
    Vieux Port 148
Cassis 81, 82–83, 85
    harbour *82*, 83
    stone 83
Le Castellet 87, 88, *88*
Cézanne, Paul 7, 49, 77

Chaîne des Alpilles 49, 51, 53, 54, *55*
Cisterians 31, 71
La Ciotat 85, *85*
    L'Eden cinema 85
Colmars-les-Alpes 122–25
    Fort de France *124*, 125
    Fort de Savoie 125
Colostre valley 138, 140
Comtat Venaissin 21, 27, 29
Corsica 91, 158
Côtes-du-Rhône 6, 8, 16
Cotignac 95, *95*
Coulon valley 34, *34*
Count of Monte Cristo 81
Counts of Toulouse 21, 25
Crau Plain 54
Crestet 21–22
    fountain 22, *22*
    Stahly foundation 21
crusades 62, 135

Dentelles de Montmirail 12, 16,
    16, 21, 22
Draguignan 87
Durance river and valley 11, 53, 54,
    71, 125

Eiffel, Gustave 158
Entrecasteaux 96, *97*
    castle 96
Entrevaux 133–35
    Cathédrale Notre-Dame-de-
        l'Assomption *134*, 135
    citadel 133
Ephrussi de Rothschild, Béatrice 163
l'Estaque 77
    church 77, *77*
l'Esterel, Massif de 87, *118*, 119, 148
Eygalières 53–54
    Chapelle des Pénitents 54, *54*
Éze 164–65
    Jardin d'Éze *164*, 165

Faron, Mont 91, 161
Ferrat, Cap 158, 163
    Villa Ephrussi de Rothschild *162*, 163
food 6, 8, 11, 121, 155

Foster, Norman 59
Fox-Amphoux *92*, 93
Fréjus 117
    Cathédrale St-Léonce baptistery
        117, *117*
    Roman remains 117
French Revolution 21, 29, 31, 49, 93

Gard 56
Gardon river 61
Gigondas 6
Gordes 11, 32–34, 38, 40
    Église St-Fermin 33
    Musée Pol Mara 33
Grimaud 109–11
    Château de Grimaud *110*, 111
    Église St-Michel 109, *109*

Haute-de-Cagnes 152, *153*
    Château Grimaldi 152
Hyères (area) 98–101
    Îles d'Hyères 87, 100, *101*, 103
    Île du Levant 99, 100
    Île de Porquerolles 99, 100
    Île de Port-Cros 99, 100
    Presqu'île de Giens *98*, 99
    Tour Fondue 99
Hyères (town) 99–100
    Collégiale St-Paul 99, *99*
    Tour St-Blaise 100, *100*

Îles de Lérins 148
L'Isle-sur-la-Sorgue 29, 29
    church of Notre-Dame-des-Anges 29
    Maison René Char 29
Italy 145, 161, 165, 173

Julius Caesar 117

Lacoste 11, 38, 40
    castle gateway *39*
    chateau of the Marquis de Sade 38
Le Lavandou *102*, 103
lavender 6, 11, 12, *13*, *30*, 38, 121,
    137, *137*
Lourmarin 40, 44–45
    Château de Lourmarin *44*, 45

Église SS-Andre et Trophime 45, *45*
Luberon 6, 11, 12, 40, 42, 45, 54
Luceram 176–78
    Chapelle St-Jean 177, *177*
    Église Ste-Marguerite *176*, 177
    Musée de la Crèche 177
Lumière brothers 85
Lurs 125–27
    chapel of Notre-Dame-de-Vie
        126, 127
    Promenade des Évêques 127

Malpasset Dam 117
Marguareis, Massif 185
Marseille 6, 9, 49, 77, 78–81
    Basilica Notre-Dame de la Garde 79
    Cathédrale de la Nouvelle Major
        79, *79*
    Île d'If 81
    Château d'If *80*, 81
    Vieux Port *78*, 79
Martigues 68, 77
    Canal Saint-Sébastien 68, *69*
Maures, Massif des 7, 103, 109
Méailles 130–33
    church *132*, 133
    Grottes de Méailles 131
Mediterranean Sea 8, 49, 68, 81, 87,
    145, 161
Ménerbes 6, 11, 34, 38
    parish church 38, *38*
Menton *172*, 173
    Basilique St-Michel Archange 173
Mercantour, Parc National du 7, 121,
    122, 129, *146*, 147
Merveilles valley 146
Meyrargues 71
    chateau 71
    Roman aqueduct *71*
Monaco 166–71
    Casino de Monte Carlo 171, *171*
    Fontvieille 166
    Monaco Cathedral *170*, 171
    Monaco-Ville 168–71
    Monte Carlo 171
    Musée Océanographique 171
    Palais Princier 168, *169*
    Place du Palais 168
    Port de Fontvieille 166, *167*
    Port Hercule 166
Morocco 6, 40
Moustiers-Ste-Marie 135–37
    Chapelle Notre-Dame de

Beauvoir 137
    church 135, *135*
    Ravin de Notre Dame *136*, 137

Napoleon 29, 100
Nice 7, 129, 145, 152, 156–61, 174
    Cathédrale Orthodoxe Russe
        160, 161
    Colline du Château 158
    Église Notre-Dame du Port 158
    Hôtel Negresco 158, *158*
    Place Garibaldi 156, 158
    Place Île de Beauté 158
    Place Messéna 156
    port 158, *159*
    Promenade des Anglais 156, *157*
    Quai Rauba Capeu 158
Nicholas II, Czar 158
Nicholas Alexandrovich, Tsarevich 161
Nîmes 49, 56–61
    Les Arènes 56, *57*, 59
    Carré d'Art 59
    Jardin de la Fontaine 59, *59*
    Maison Carrée *58*, 59
    Pont du Gard *60*, 61
    Temple of Diana 59
    Tour Magne 59
Nostradamus 67

Oppède-de-Vieux 34
    church of Notre-Dame-d'Alydon
        34, *35*
Orange 11
    Roman theatre 11
Ouvèze river 16, *17*
    Roman bridge 16

Pampelonne bay and beach 103,
    108, 109
Paris 8, 9, 106, 171
Peillon 174–75
    Chapelle des Pénitents Blancs 174
    Église St-Sauveur de la
        Transfiguration 174, *175*
pétanque 85, 106
popes 6, 29, 40, 173

Ramatuelle 103–05
    Le Moulin de Paillas *104*, 105
René, Good King 51, 75
Rhône river and valley 12, 16, 49, 51,
    53, 61, 65
Riez 138–42

cathedral 138
    Chapelle Ste-Maxime 140, *141*,
        142, *142*
Riviera, French 7, 87, 145
Roaix 25
Rogue-d'Anthéron 71
    Abbaye de Silvacane *70*, 71
Roman heritage 6, 11, 73, 152
Roman remains 16, 42, 49, 59, 61, 62,
    71, 93, 117
Roussillon *36*, 37, 40
    ochre quarries 37, *37*
    Sentier des Ocres 37
La Roya valley 178, *179*, 182

Salon-de-Provence 67
    Église St-Michel 67, *67*
    Musée Nostradamus 67
Sanary-sur-Mer *90*, 91
    Chapelle Notre-Dame-de-Pieté 91
Saorge 178–83
    Chapelle de la Madone del Poggio
        181, 182, *183*
    Couvent Franciscain 181, *181*
Sardinia 91
Sault 12
    lavender fields 12, *13*
Savoie 133, 177
Second World War 9, 81, 109, 181, 187
Séguret 22–25
    poppy field *24*, 25
    church of St-Denis 22, *23*
Seillans 116, 117
Sorgue river 29
spa/spring 73, 93
St-Benoît 131
St-Paul-de-Vence *154*, 155
    Fondation Maeght 155
St-Rémy-de-Provence 7
    St-Paul-de-Mausole asylum 7
St-Tropez 7, 87, 105, 106, *107*, 109,
    117, 165
    Place Carnot 106
Statue of Liberty 83
Ste-Baume, Massif 88
Ste-Cassien lake 87, 115
Ste-Croix lake 87, 115, 121, 142
Ste-Victoire, Montagne 7, 47, 49, *76*, 77

Tarascon 51
    Château du Roi René *50*, 51
Templar Knights 95, 100
Le Tholonet 77

cathedral 138
Toulon 87, 91, *91*
    Cathédrale Notre-Dame-de-la-Seds
        91
    Jardin Alexander Ier 91
    Marché Provençal 91
    Opéra 91
    Place de la Liberté 91
Tour de France 12
Tourtour 93, *93*, 95
Trigance 115, *115*
    chateau 115

Ubaye valley 7, 121
UNESCO 12, 61

Vacqueyras 6
Vaire river and valley 129, *129*, 131
Vaison-la-Romaine 11, 16–21
    ancient ruins 16
    castle 21
    Cathédrale Notre-Dame-de-Nazereth
        19
    parish church *18*, 19
    Quartier Puymin 16, 19
    Quartier de la Villasse 16, 19
    St-Quenin chapel 19
Van Gogh, Vincent 7, 49, 62
Var 7, 86–119
Vaucluse 6, 8, 10–47, 49
Vaucluse, Monts de 40
Vaucluse, Plateau de 27, 29, 34, 37, 38
Valensole (town) 137
Valensole, Plateau de 121, 137, *137*,
    138, 142
    church of St Blaise 137
Venasque *26*, 27
    church of Notre Dame 27
Ventoux, Mont 6, 11, 12, *12*, 14, 21, 40
Verdon, Gorges du 7, 115, 121, 129, 135,
    142, *143*
Verdon river and valley 121, 125, 142
Villecroze 95
    commanderie 95
    St-Victor chapel 95
Villefranche-sur-Mer 161, *161*, 163
    Canyon of Villefranche 161
    Chapelle St-Pierre 161
    Citadelle St-Elme 161
    Fort du Mont Alban 161
Vinaigre, Mont 119

wine 8, 25, 87, 88, 111, 155